EXPLORING BRITAIN

◆

A Regional Guide:
Places to go, things to do

◆

FRONT COVER PICTURES
Main picture: The Wye Valley
Inset, left to right: The River Cam,
Cambridge.
Chessington World of Adventures.
Bamburgh Castle.

BACK COVER PICTURE
Polperro, Cornwall

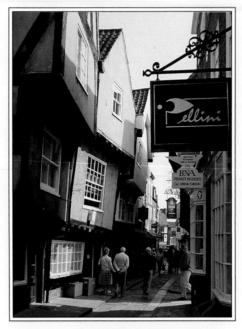

The Shambles, York.

Opposite Page *Stratford-upon-Avon.*

EXPLORING BRITAIN
A Regional Guide:
Places to go, things to do

Text copyright © Jarrold Publishing 1991
This edition copyright © Jarrold Publishing 1991

This edition specially produced for
W H Smith Limited
Greenbridge Road Swindon SN3 3LD
by Jarrold Publishing, Norwich

Designed and produced by Parke Sutton Limited, Norwich
for Jarrold Publishing, Norwich

ISBN 0-7117-0491-0

Printed and bound in Hong Kong

EXPLORING BRITAIN

A Regional Guide: Places to go, things to do

WHSMITH

EXCLUSIVE
· BOOKS ·

CONTRIBUTORS

Authors
Penny Tripp
Angela Martin

Editor
Lucy Stone

Designer
Sue Goodrum

The Gardens at Athelhampton, Dorset.

• CONTENTS •

• FOREWORD •

Those of us who are fortunate enough to live in Britain are aware that we cannot boast of the country's great size, of the length of its rivers, the height of its mountains or the largeness of its lakes. Britain is a comparatively small island, and its geographical features, like its climate, do not tend to the extremes. What we do claim, however, is that within its compass is an unrivalled variety of landscape and places of interest. Historic towns and cities with ancient houses and churches at every turn; magnificent castles redolent with hundreds of years of fascinating history; beautiful gardens and glorious countryside; as well as an amazing choice of museums and other tourist attractions. Truly there is something for everyone and for every occasion.

Of course, no single book can contain them all, so when planning this volume's contents we approached the staff of our regional tourist boards – the experts on their particular region of Britain. We asked them not only to tell us about the famous sites in

their part of the country – those places which are a must for visitors to see – but also about the less well-known places, that they with their insider's knowledge might take a personal friend or visitor to see – places away from the hustle and bustle of the beaten track, but no less worthwhile for all that. I am happy to acknowledge here the help and advice given to the publisher by the national tourist boards of Scotland and Wales, and the regional tourist boards of England.

So here, in *Exploring Britain*, is a selection of all that is best about the regions of Britain in their magnificent abundance, illustrated throughout with superb photographs. I would venture to say that it is a book for residents (who often do not realise what glories they have on their doorsteps!) as much as for tourists from overseas, and it will be invaluable for planning tours or individual days out. But besides its usefulness as a work of reference I hope that you will find this a book to linger over, a souvenir perhaps, which will enable you once more to experience the wonders of Britain.

Richard Cowles, British Tourist Authority

The River Stour, Canterbury, Kent

• ACKNOWLEDGMENTS •

The majority of photographs in this book were provided by
photographic libraries at the British Tourist Authority and Jarrold Publishing.
Others supplied to us or requiring acknowledgment are listed below.

11 By permission of Abbotsbury Swannery. 17 The National Shire Horse
Centre. 19, 20 By permission of Longleat House. 21 The Model Village,
Babbacombe. 22 Mrs Gibbs, Sheldon Manor. 23 Fleet Air Arm Museum. 25 By
permission of the National Trust. 26 R.J. Sheppy & Son. 28 Tutenkhamun:
the exhibition. 29 Winchester City Council. 36 Longdown Dairy Farm.
39 Paultons Park. 40 Winchester City Council. 41 Mid-Hants Railway.
43, 44 © Nigh, Shanklin, I.W. 47 By permission of Blenheim Palace.
48 Bekonscot Model Village. 50 Mill Green Museum and Mill. 54 Courage
Shire Horse Centre. 55 Beale Bird Park. 56 Capel Manor. 58 By permission of
Woburn Abbey. 63 Chessington World of Adventures. 65, 66 Southern Water
Services Ltd. 67 Goodwood House. 70, 71 The Royal Pavilion, Art Gallery
and Museums. 72 Whitbread Hop Farm. 74, 75 By permission of The Royal
Horticultural Society. 76 Tangmere Military Aviation Museum Trust. 76 The
Bluebell Railway. 77 Arundel Toy and Military Museum. 78 Buckleys Shop
Museum. 91 By permission of Sandringham House. 92 Ickworth. 135 *top*
Anglesey Sea Zoo; *right* Museum of Childhood. 154 Oakwood Adventure and
Leisure Park. 156 Stuart and Sons Ltd. 163 Speedwell Cavern Ltd. 164 The
Boat Museum Trust. 169 Jodrell Bank. 172 *below, right* Stapeley Water
Gardens. 173 Museum of Science and Industry. 175 By permission of
Knowsley Safari Park. 176 *above* Leighton Hall; *below* The Last Drop Village.
177 Norton Priory Museum. 185 National Museum of Film, Photography and
Television. 189 Yorkshire Mining Museum. 202 Lowther Leisure Park.
207 Penrith Steam Museum. 212 The Wildfowl and Wetlands Trust. 213 By
permission of Raby Castle. 214 Alnwick Castle. 215 The North of England
Open Air Museum. 219 St Mary's Lighthouse. 220 Preston Park Museum.
221 Gateshead MetroCentre. 223 Heatherslaw Light Railway Co. Ltd. 225,
226 City Engineer, Newcastle. 230 Highland Folk Museum. 231 By
permission of Balmoral. 235 Aberdeen Tourist Board. 237 Mull Little Theatre.

Special thanks also go to Piers
for designing the regional maps.

WEST COUNTRY

Polperro, Cornwall

The west country is a land steeped in history and legend. The village of Avebury in Wiltshire is the site of Neolithic Stone Circles, Bath in Avon has the best Roman remains in Britain, and legend claims that Glastonbury in Somerset is the burial place of the legendary King Arthur.

Castle building was prolific in the west country during the Norman Conquest when many were built to control the natives. Even today some villages, such as Launceston, are overshadowed by these huge castles. Fortresses were also built along the coastline which covers a stretch of some 650 miles, to guard against invasion.

The west country is also a land of mystery. At Tintagel Castle Arthur was said to have held court, while close by, in Wiltshire, stands Stonehenge – a construction which still defies complete explanation.

The mild southerly climate is ideal for agriculture, and the growth of early fruit and vegetables. Horticulture is popular around the county and sub-tropical vegetation flourishes in the mild climate. The area also contains what is thought to be the first English garden at Chysauster Ancient Village (near Penzance) in the courtyard of some 2000 year old Iron Age houses.

The area has its own unique and varied natural beauty. In Somerset there is the geological beauty of Cheddar Gorge, in Cornwall the tiny bays, fishing villages and rugged hills of Bodmin Moor. Devon embraces the wide wild stretches of the national park of Dartmoor which comprises rolling granite hills rising to tors – the highest is 2039 feet – and the heather and bracken of Exmoor – the home of Lorna Doone. Exmoor is also home to ponies, red deer, foxes, badgers and sheep.

The dairy industry has a long tradition in the area and local delicacies are both delicious and wholesome. Devonshire and Cornish clotted cream are found here, as is cheddar cheese, for this is the county of the traditional Cheddar. Locally made cider, and scrumpy, are a must, and visitors should not miss the salmon and trout from the River Tamar. Not forgetting Cornish pasties, that never taste quite the same anywhere else!

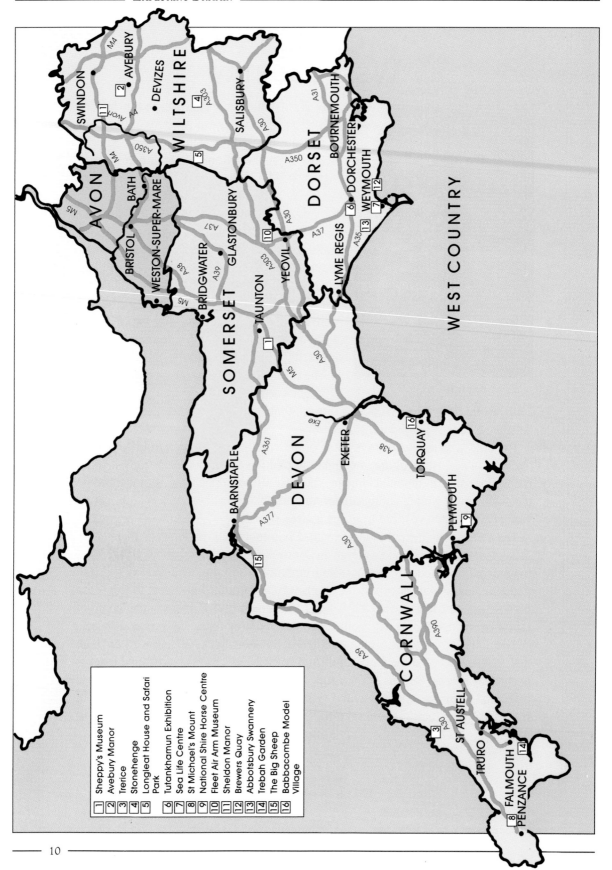

SWINDON

M4

AVEBURY

2

DEVIZES

4

A303

SALISBURY

WILTSHIRE

11

AVON

A4

A350

M4

5

BOURNEMOUTH

A31

M5

BATH

A350

DORSET

DORCHESTER

WEYMOUTH

12

BRISTOL

WESTON-SUPER-MARE

A37

GLASTONBURY

6

7

A30

LYME REGIS

13

A35

A38

A39

YEOVIL

10

A37

A30

BRIDGWATER

SOMERSET

TAUNTON

A303

M5

1

WEST COUNTRY

A30

M5

Exe

EXETER

16

DEVON

A38

TORQUAY

BARNSTAPLE

A361

A377

PLYMOUTH

9

A30

CORNWALL

A390

A39

ST AUSTELL

15

3

A30

TRURO

FALMOUTH

14

8

PENZANCE

1	Sheppy's Museum
2	Avebury Manor
3	Trerice
4	Stonehenge
5	Longleat House and Safari Park
6	Tutankhamun Exhibition
7	Sea Life Centre
8	St Michael's Mount
9	National Shire Horse Centre
10	Fleet Air Arm Museum
11	Sheldon Manor
12	Brewers Quay
13	Abbotsbury Swannery
14	Trebah Garden
15	The Big Sheep
16	Babbacombe Model Village

ABBOTSBURY SWANNERY
Abbotsbury, Dorset

There have been swans at Abbotsbury since the 14th century, when they were introduced by the monks who occupied the Benedictine Abbey of St Peter. Their home since then, known as the Fleet, has been a unique nine-mile-long lagoon separated from the open sea by Chesil Beach. As well as the swans, visitors here can see a working reed-bed, which supplies the raw material for thatchers in the area. The site is open to the public from May until September.

Only the ruins of the 12th-century Benedictine abbey now remain in the village, but the 15th-century church of St Nicholas was once part of it – and so was the great tithe barn, built around the year 1400, and 276 feet long.

Taking advantage of some freakish climatic conditions resulting from its own sheltered position, and not far away from the Swannery, the beautiful Abbotsbury Sub-

Abbotsbury has been home to the world famous herd of Mute Swans since the 14th century.

Tropical Gardens (open March to October) cover twenty acres of the English countryside with exotic trees and shrubs.

BATH Avon

Superb Roman remains and a wealth of fine Georgian architecture combine to make Bath one of England's most elegant cities. Its compact centre – broad main streets linked by narrow, traffic-free lanes – makes it easy to explore on foot.

Twelve hundred years after the Romans left Britain in the 5th century, the therapeutic baths they built at the town they called Aquae Sulis were rediscovered. Their Great Bath, with its original lead lining, was only found 100 years ago. Still fed by underground mineral springs producing 250,000 gallons of warm water every day, the baths lie within a complex that is Britain's greatest memorial – after Hadrian's Wall – to its long-gone conquerors. Below street-level in the centre of town, the restored baths and a nearby museum contain relics of the Romans and Bath's history in general.

Though beautiful Bath Abbey – sometimes called 'The Lantern of the West' because of its enormous clear glass windows – was built at the end of the 15th century, it was not until the early 1700s that the spa enjoyed its great revival as a centre of high fashion and good taste. Massive rebuilding schemes replaced much of the medieval city with the golden Georgian terraces made from locally-quarried Bath stone that remain today.

The city centre's elegant houses line spacious thoroughfares. The Circus, Queen Square and Royal Crescent are the best known: 1, Royal Crescent has been restored by the Bath Preservation Society, furnished in period and opened to the public. Other fine 18th-century buildings include The Pump Room, Bath's social centre in Nash's time (though since rebuilt) and still a popular meeting-place, The Guildhall and The Assembly Rooms. The latter now houses the

The ancient Roman central heating system, the hypocaust, where hot air circulated beneath the floor (top, right). The therapeutic baths are still fed by underground mineral springs (below, right and opposite page).

BATH

The Bath that Jane Austen wrote of still remains largely unchanged. Bath in bloom (top, left); the Circus (top, right); Lansdowne Crescent (above); the Assembly Rooms (below, right); Bath Abbey (below, left).

Museum of Costume, one of the largest of its kind in the world.

Also recapturing the past are The Carriage Museum, housed in stables and coach-houses behind The Circus; Burrows Toy Museum, covering 200 years of children's amusements; and the Holburne of Menstrie Museum, with its collections of important 18th-century silver, porcelain and paintings. Art of a different kind altogether is on display at the Museum of English Naïve Art, where the Crane Kalman Collection hangs in The Countess of Huntingdon Chapel. Eight miles out of town, Claverton Manor is the home of the American Museum in Britain, covering American domestic life from the 17th–19th centuries.

Parks and gardens throughout the city set off the formality of the Georgian architecture. The wooded Victoria Park, not far from Royal Crescent, has an important botanical garden as well as a children's playground.

The highlight of the city's thriving cultural life comes in June when the Bath Festival features plays, ballet, exhibitions, lectures and – most famously – music.

The Parade Gardens, Bath.

Glastonbury Abbey, the first Christian sanctuary in the British Isles, is the legendary burial place of King Arthur (right). Extensive ruins still remain of the abbey (below), which is reputed to have been founded by Joseph of Arimathea in the 1st century.

GLASTONBURY Somerset

Legend has it that the chalice used at the Last Supper was buried on the slopes of Glastonbury Tor by Joseph of Arimathea, one of the first Christian missionaries to arrive in Britain from the Holy Land. It is also said that a sign from God led him to found a monastery here on the site of what was to become the great abbey whose remains still exist today. Later stories connect the area with Arthurian legend – the chalice became the Holy Grail sought by Arthur's knights, and he and his wife Guinevere are said to be buried in the abbey.

Whatever the truth, there is no doubt that Glastonbury has a mystery and magic all its own. The Tor, topped by a 14th-century church tower, can be seen from miles away, rising majestically from the plain in which it stands. At the time of the Crucifixion it would have been an island surrounded by marshes and lakes.

Joseph's original wattle-and-daub church became one of the richest and most beautiful monasteries in the land; from the 7th century – as now – the site was a centre for pilgrims. Only fragments survive (in the Medieval Gatehouse Museum), but the present ruins come from the abbey which replaced it in the 13th century. Two of the buildings remain intact: the kitchens, now containing a museum, and the 14th-century Abbot's Barn. The whole of the well-maintained site is informatively sign-posted, and open all year round except for Christmas Day.

Glastonbury's High Street also boasts some historic buildings. St John's Church, with its exceptionally fine tower, was built in the 15th century, and contains a tomb once thought to be that of Joseph of Arimathea. A museum containing finds from the lake-villages where local marsh-dwellers once lived is housed in the 15th-century tribunal abbey court-house. The George Inn was built in the 15th century as a resting place for pilgrims.

For 600 years until the 19th century, Glastonbury was a thriving wool centre, and its key industries are still related to the production of sheepskin and leather goods.

National Shire Horse Centre
Yealmpton, near Plymouth, Devon

Although it is years since tractors replaced Shire horses as the main source of power on farms up and down the country, the animals' dignified beauty, strength and placidity has meant that they still hold a very special place in many people's hearts. At the National Shire Horse Centre over 30 adult horses and their foals are in residence and on display.

Throughout the summer months (March to October) the horses are on parade daily and there are a number of special events. Current ones include country and medieval fairs, garden festivals and steam rallies, though details and dates (available from the Centre) vary from year to year. During the winter the stables, shops, craft centre and restaurant are still open, but there are no shows or parades.

There are plenty of play facilities for children at the Centre, and they have the chance to get really close to a variety of animals and birds in the pets' area and petting paddocks. Hawks, owls, buzzards and other birds of prey are on show, and spectacular flying displays (Easter–October) are held at the Falconry Centre.

Horses are on parade daily during the summer months at the National Shire Horse Centre.

STONEHENGE *Near Amesbury, Wiltshire*

Those who started to build Stonehenge lived around 5000 years ago, at the very end of the prehistoric Neolithic period, and their work was not completed for another four centuries. What remains today is widely reckoned to be the finest Bronze Age monument in Europe, and there is nothing quite like it anywhere else in the world.

Building seems to have taken place in phases. Around 1800 BC a ditch and bank were constructed, inside which was a ring of small pits. Some evidence suggests that these may have been burial places. A few upright stones were erected, possibly to form an entrance to the site. Various modifications and additions, involving bluestones from south Wales as well as great sarsens from the Marlborough Downs twenty miles away, were made over the next four centuries. The present arrangement of stones – the remains of two circles of sarsens, some weighing over 50 tons, with an inner horseshoe of bluestones – is what was left after medieval builders used the site as a source of stone for their own constructions.

Nobody knows why Stonehenge was built.

An apparent link between the orientation of the stones and the position of the sun at midsummer and midwinter suggests that it had something to do with the changing seasons; other evidence points to a connection with the monthly lunar cycle. Whether its function was temporal or, as others believe, religious will probably never be fully understood.

Also impossible to grasp is how its prehistoric builders could have transported, worked and erected the huge stones that were their raw materials. The massive lintels topping the uprights are actually mortice-and-tenoned into place, and curved to follow the circumference of their circle.

The mystery that is Stonehenge is accessible to visitors every day of the year.

LONGLEAT HOUSE AND SAFARI PARK *Warminster, Wiltshire*

One of the great surviving examples of Elizabethan architecture, and the first stately home in England to open its doors to the public, Longleat House is set in gardens that were originally landscaped by Capability Brown. Magnificent state rooms contain fine

The awe-inspiring mystery of Stonehenge (opposite page).

Longleat House was the first stately home to open its doors to the public 40 years ago.

furniture and paintings; libraries, kitchens, the Great Hall and state dining room are all on show, as are other areas of the house.

Longleat is also known for its Safari Park, the first in the world to open outside Africa. Wild animals, some of them representatives of endangered species, roam freely through the Park: the collection includes rhinos, hippos, elephants, gorillas, giraffes and zebras. The famous Longleat lions have now been joined by a group of Bengal tigers — including the only white tiger in Britain — to form the largest collection of big cats in Europe. Visitors can tour the Park in their own cars (except soft-tops), or join one of the special safari buses.

Inanimate attractions include the world's largest maze, the children's Adventure Castle playpark, and trips on a narrow-gauge railway.

Longleat House is open all year except for Christmas Day, while the Safari Park welcomes visitors between early March and the end of October.

Visitors experience the atmosphere of Africa at Longleat Safari Park (below).

AVEBURY *Wiltshire*

Surrounding the present-day village of Avebury is what is left of the largest complex of stone circles in the world. No-one knows why it was erected about 4000 years ago, though it is thought to have been an important ceremonial centre of some kind: fear that the stones had pagan significance accounts for the fact that many were felled and buried in the Middle Ages. It was at this time, too, that a village first grew up among the stones.

The Avebury circles are related to a number of other prehistoric constructions in the area: a double avenue of stones, for example, once ran all the way to other circles at Overton Hill, more than a mile away to the east, and has now been partially restored.

Finds from archaeological excavations at Avebury and the other prehistoric sites nearby – West Kennet Long Barrow, Silbury Hill and Windmill Hill – are displayed at Avebury's Alexander Keiller Museum, headquarters during the 1930s of the archaeologist responsible for excavating half of Avebury's outer circle.

The village's more recent history is celebrated at Avebury Manor (open March–October, which dates from Elizabethan times and now houses some fine collections displayed in period settings. The 17th-century Great Barn, where there are regular programmes of craft demonstrations and displays of a number of rural crafts, is open daily between March and October, and at weekends during the winter.

MODEL VILLAGE
Babbacombe, Torquay, Devon

In a sustained masterpiece of miniature landscaping, the many facets of the English countryside have been re-created on a four-acre site at Babbacombe Model Village.

A village, complete with thatched buildings and its own stately home, exemplifies the traditional rural face of England; a

Lord Elpus Hall, at Babbacombe Model Village.

modern town, with its traffic-crowded high street, brings the picture up to date.

Set amidst award-winning gardens – including a lake, waterfalls and a unique collection of dwarf conifers – the Model Village is open all year, though times vary according to the season. From Easter to mid-October, when the site can be visited until 10pm, it is illuminated from dusk onwards.

SEA LIFE CENTRE
Lodmoor Country Park, Weymouth, Dorset

Close encounters with hundreds of sea-creatures can be experienced at the Sea Life Centre, where living displays of a wealth of underwater marine life can be visited all year.

Thousands of gallons of water surround visitors as they come face-to-face with exotic sea-dwellers such as octopus, vicious trigger fish, catfish, lobsters and sting-rays. Sharks from the Pacific Ocean cruise past at eye-level. The Ocean Tunnel recreates the sensation of being underwater surrounded by shimmering shoals of fish; scuba-diving displays during July and August (conditions permitting) are also on the menu. Specially-designed rock pools make an ideal environment for a variety of sea-creatures usually only found in the wild around the coast of Britain.

The timing of feeding displays and talks varies: contact the Centre for details.

Other facilities on site include plenty of activities for children (including a splash-pool), a restaurant and lakeside picnic area, and a gift shop.

SHELDON MANOR
Near Chippenham, Wiltshire

Wiltshire's oldest inhabited manor house, apparently the sole survivor of what was once a medieval village, has been lived in for 700 years.

Its significant architectural features include a 13th-century porch and 15th-century chapel, while among the treasures to see inside are collections of early English oak furniture, porcelain, Nailsea glass and Persian saddle-bags. The gardens surrounding the manor have ancient yew trees, and a profusion of old-fashioned roses bloom in June and July.

Visitors are welcome on selected afternoons between Easter and the end of September, and can wander the manor unhindered by roped-off areas. Parties can be catered for at any time, but only by prior arrangement. Refreshments are available in the form of home-made buffet lunches and cream teas.

THE FLEET AIR ARM MUSEUM
Royal Naval Air Station, Yeovilton, Somerset

Designed to appeal to children and adults alike, the exhibits at the Fleet Air Arm Museum are more than just a series of static displays. The emphasis is on recapturing some of the adventure and romance associated with aviation's short history in peacetime and in war – and the fact that the museum is sited on a working air station means that visitors can see some of the latest aircraft actually in action.

One of the world's largest collections of historic aircraft includes Concorde 002, the British-assembled prototype of one of the most glamorous passenger planes ever.

Sheldon Manor is Wiltshire's oldest inhabited manor house. It is all that remains of what was once a medieval village.

Visitors can walk through the aircraft, explore its cockpit, and – also in the Concorde Exhibition Hall – trace the development of supersonic flight.

Wartime planes in the museum include flying replicas of the Sopwith Pup, the Sopwith Camel and Albatros DVa, as well as a selection of World War Two bombers. Hundreds of weapons, uniforms, photographs, models and memorabilia pay tribute to the pilots whose job it was to safeguard Britain's interests from World War One to the Falklands conflict. Other displays feature the aircraft of the jet age, and the continuing story of the Women's Royal Air Service.

Children of all ages can learn what it is like to fly in a variety of craft by taking a trip in the 'Super X' experience simulator, and travel as far as their imagination can take them at the controls of their own plane.

All facilities are under cover and open year round (except Christmas Eve, Christmas Day and Boxing Day), though times vary with the season.

The Fairey Fulmer (above) and the Westland-Sikorsky Dragonfly (right) at Fleet Air Arm Museum.

ST MICHAEL'S MOUNT
Near Marazion, Cornwall

It is no coincidence that St Michael's Mount so strikingly resembles Mont St Michel off the Normandy coast: both were orginally chosen as monastery sites by monks from the same Benedictine order.

Unfortunately for the monks, however – and the Priory they built – St Michael's potential as a fortification attracted the attention of English kings and their rebellious nobles: in 1425 they were thrown out, their property was taken over by the Crown, and the Priory became a fine castle. It remained a military stronghold from 1193 until the mid-17th century, when it was bought by the St Aubyn family whose descendants still live there.

Rich reminders of its varied past still exist on St Michael's Mount. The present church there dates from the 14th century, while within the castle itself, the Chevy Chase Room was once the monks' refectory. Later occupants created the 18th-century Blue Drawing Rooms, decorated them in the style known as 'Strawberry Hill Gothic' and furnished them with fine pieces of Chippendale. Paintings by notable artists hang throughout the property. Collections of weapons, maps, 18th-century clothes and family silver are displayed in the Armoury, Map Room and Museum Room: one interesting oddity is a model of the Mount carved out of champagne corks by a pre-war butler.

High tide submerges the causeway that links St Michael's Mount to the mainland, though regular ferryboats (except in winter) make the journey when foot travel is impossible. The National Trust, which has owned the site since 1954, runs a Tourist Centre where visitors can learn more about the castle's history. The castle itself is open between the beginning of April and the end of October, though guided tours can be arranged by prior appointment during the winter months.

TRERICE Near Newquay, Cornwall

Trerice has experienced relatively little alteration since it was built in 1573 by Sir John Arundell, member of a famous Cornish family. He may have been inspired by buildings he saw while soldiering in the Low Countries, for some features – like the curving Dutch gables on the house's silvery-grey façade – are not found on any other west country properties of the same period.

Though Elizabethan, the house is based on a pattern common in medieval times. Its Hall rises through two storeys and is lit by a huge window containing almost 600 panes of glass – many of them original. In common with some other Cornish properties of the time, elaborate plasterwork ceilings and fire-

St Michael's Mount (opposite page) was a Benedictine monastery and a military stronghold before becoming the family home that it still is today.

Trerice was built according to the traditional plan of an English manor house.

places are a feature of the house and it has been suggested that the same master craftsman – perhaps introduced to his neighbours by Sir John Arundell – was responsible for all of them.

Fine 17th- and 18th-century oak and walnut furniture is displayed throughout the house, and there are collections of porcelain and china from Europe and the Far East.

Outside, the Great Barn to the west of the house is of a size and age rarely found in Cornwall. It is thought to date from the 15th century and now houses the restaurant run by the National Trust, who have managed the property since 1954. An unusual collection of lawn-mowers is displayed in what used to be the hayloft of the former stables.

SHEPPY'S MUSEUM
Bradford-on-Tone, near Taunton, Somerset

Though the days when every Somerset farm made its own cider are long gone, cider-making has a long tradition in the county. In the Vale of Taunton Deane, the Sheppy family has been growing apples and processing the harvest into one of the West Country's most famous drinks for close on 200 years.

Today, 42 acres of cider orchards produce apples with romantic names like Kingston Black, Yarlington Mill and Tremlett's Bitter which are turned, each autumn, into award-winning ciders. Sheppy's modern Press Room is open to visitors, as is the Farm and Cider Museum which houses antique agricultural and cider equipment as well as the tools of coopers and other craftsmen whose work was important to the cider-maker.

Sheppy's is open year-round, though times vary according to the day of the week and the season. Pre-booked parties of twenty or more have the chance to see a slide-show on the art of cider-making.

Cider has been made at Sheppy's since the early 19th century.

THE BIG SHEEP
Abbotsham, near Bideford, North Devon

There have been sheep on the hillsides in Abbotsham since monks farmed them there around 700 years ago. Nowadays, eighteen acres of one family's farmland – the rest is given over to a 500-ewe commercial sheep farm – have been transformed into The Big Sheep which, since it opened in 1988, has won two of England's most prestigious awards for tourism.

Demonstrations of shearing, dipping and milking are open to the public, and visitors can get involved in many of the activities – like spinning and weaving – that take place in the Woolcraft Centre. One of the first working sheep dairies in England is open to view, and its products – milk, yoghurt, cheese, fudge and ice cream – are on sale.

Open from Easter until October, The Big Sheep offers the chance to see the serious side of sheep-keeping as well as some of the traditional skills involved in shepherding. Some demonstrations depend on the cooperation of the weather.

There are plenty of lighter moments, too – including sheep racing – but, again, the weather may well determine the timing of specific events. Souvenirs, ranging from salt and pepper pots to knitwear, are on sale.

BREWERS QUAY Weymouth, Dorset

Centrepiece of an ambitious regeneration scheme for the historic quayside area of old Weymouth, Brewers Quay lies just off the harbour which – until 1781 – stretched as far as the town's square.

Former malthouses and other imposing buildings have been converted into a development which mixes residential and commercial properties – including 20,000 square feet of speciality shopping, workshop, restaurant, bar and exhibition facilities.

New streets and alleyways, bordered by small shops, are grouped in themed areas,

Weymouth harbour now incorporates Brewers Quay, centrepiece of a unique scheme to regenerate a historic part of old Weymouth.

but Brewers Quay aims to be more than just another place where people go to shop. Its Timewalk takes visitors back to Weymouth's past, dramatically reconstructing historical events and their settings. The horrors of the Black Death, the area's seafaring and smuggling connections, and the splendour of Georgian high society are all vividly portrayed.

There are reminders, too, of Brewers Quay's own origins: Timewalk takes in the listed interiors of the old brewery, complete with re-created cooper's and signwriter's shops.

TREBAH GARDEN
Near Falmouth, Cornwall

The 25-acre Trebah Garden clothes the wooded sides of a 500-yard ravine that falls 200 feet towards the estuary of the Helford River. Charles Fox, who started planting it in the 19th century, was one of a family who created many great gardens in the area and brought seeds and plants here from all over the world. A number of fine gardeners had a hand in Trebah's development for its first 100 years, but it had been sadly neglected by the time its present owners took over in 1981.

Recent plantings have been designed to complement the original landscaping, and work continues. Trebah's own nurseries are involved in propagating rare and exotic plants both for use in the gardens and for sale to the public.

Sign-posted walks lead visitors through glades of huge sub-tropical tree ferns and palms, under giant rhododendrons, and past two acres of hydrangeas. A stream cascades over waterfalls, through ponds full of Koi carp, down to Trebah's private beach on the Helford estuary.

Exotic plants from all over the world combine to create a riot of colour, especially in spring and early summer, though the gardens are open all year round. Visitors are free to enjoy swimming, sunbathing and picnics on Trebah's private beach, and special play areas in the gardens cater for the needs of young children.

TUTANKHAMUN: THE EXHIBITION
Dorchester, Dorset

Tutankhamun became Pharoah of Egypt at the age of twelve, and died only six years later. The magnificent tomb at Thebes, where he was buried in about 1340 BC, was discovered in 1922 by Lord Carnarvon and Howard Carter: their experience is re-created in the spectacular exhibition which is open every day in Dorchester.

Set in a perfect reconstruction of the tomb itself, the exhibition covers the discovery of the tomb – complete with the sights, sounds and smells which accompanied it. Visitors can walk through the ante-chamber, witness the raising of the golden coffins, and see superb facsimiles of the many treasures found on the site.

Tutankhamun's magnificent tomb, dating from 1340 BC, was only discovered in 1922.

FOR FURTHER INFORMATION CONTACT:

Tourist Information Centre
Abbey Church Yard
BATH
Avon BA1 1LY
Telephone: (0225) 462831

Tourist Information Centre
The Library
Corporation Street
TAUNTON
Somerset TA1 4AN
Telephone: (0823) 274785/270479

West Country Tourist Board
37 Southernhay East
EXETER
Devon EX1 1QS
Telephone: (0392) 76351

SOUTH

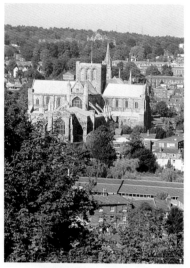

Winchester Cathedral.

The counties of Dorset and Hampshire cover an expansive stretch of the exposed southern coast which for centuries has been used as a garrison for the protection of Britain, and Portsmouth in Hampshire has been the centre of the British navy since 1540.

In order to create a stronghold many fortifications were built, and the remains of ancient castles and walled coastal forts, still standing, include Corfe and Southsea Castle. The Isle of Wight – separated from the mainland by the Solent and Spithead – was also used as a defence for the mainland. In 1853 Yarmouth Castle and Fort Victoria were built by Henry VIII as protection for Portsmouth.

As well as a heavy naval presence, the area incorporates Aldershot which became the only completely military town built since Roman times and was the main base for the Canadian Army. Today it is Britain's chief garrison town and army training centre.

Present-day visitors can relive the glories of past battles in the many military museums scattered around the counties including the Aldershot Military Museum, the Museum of Army Flying at Middle Wallop Stockbridge, and the Southampton Hall of Aviation.

The administrative centre of Hampshire is Winchester, a city which was home to Saxon Kings, and once rivalled London for supremacy as capital. Indeed the area has nurtured many famous historic people and some of their country houses are open to the public. These include Broadlands at Romsey – home to Louis Mountbatten – and Jane Austen's house at Chawton.

As well as being rich in social and military history the area is one of wild natural beauty. Hampshire is the famous watercress area and some of the wildest natural beauty can be found deep in the historic New Forest – the hunting ground of past kings. The forest survives today and consists chiefly of beech and oak woodlands, evergreen forests and open heathland.

The southerly climate and fertile lands make this an important farming area. The Isle of Wight has several vineyards and connoisseurs can sample wine at Barton Manor, and Adgestone vineyards. As an agricultural area there is a wide variety of farm produce available such as locally made cider, stoneground wholemeal flours, farmhouse cheeses – including the Dorset Blue Vinney and Somerset Brie – butter, honey, jam, jellies and preserves.

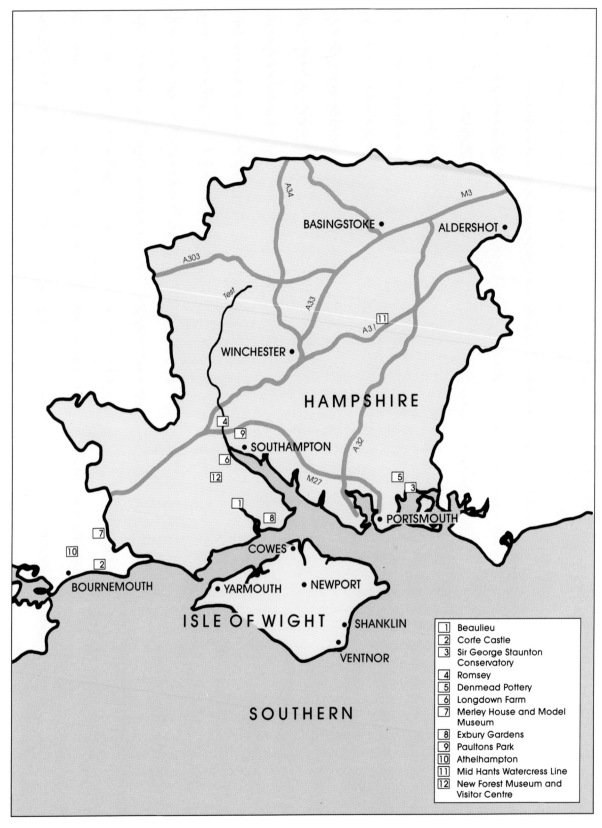

BASINGSTOKE •

ALDERSHOT •

A34

M3

A303

Test

A33

A31

11

WINCHESTER •

HAMPSHIRE

4

9

SOUTHAMPTON •

6

A32

12

5

M27

3

1

8

PORTSMOUTH •

7

COWES •

10

NEWPORT •

2

YARMOUTH •

BOURNEMOUTH •

SHANKLIN •

ISLE OF WIGHT

VENTNOR •

SOUTHERN

1	Beaulieu
2	Corfe Castle
3	Sir George Staunton Conservatory
4	Romsey
5	Denmead Pottery
6	Longdown Farm
7	Merley House and Model Museum
8	Exbury Gardens
9	Paultons Park
10	Athelhampton
11	Mid Hants Watercress Line
12	New Forest Museum and Visitor Centre

PORTSMOUTH Hampshire

Richard the Lion Heart was the first monarch to conceive the importance of Portsea Island as a strategic defence base for the English Channel and in 1194 he ordered the first docks to be built. These were increased over the centuries by succeeding monarchs and in 1540 Henry VIII expanded them further to create the first royal dockyards. At that time the docks covered about eight acres; today they extend over 300 acres.

Since those early beginnings Portsmouth has been home to many great admirals and heroes – among them Vice Admiral Nelson. Visitors to the city can see relics of Lord Nelson, his officers and men at the Victory Museum which stands in the oldest part of the dockyards.

The city has also played host to literary geniuses including Sir Arthur Conan Doyle who established a surgery in Portsea, H. G. Wells who worked as a drapery assistant on the corner of King's Road, George Meredith, Rudyard Kipling, Nevil Shute and Charles Dickens, born in 1812 in a house in Commercial Road. The house is now a Dickens Museum containing personal relics and an extensive library of his works.

Southsea Castle was also built by Henry VIII in 1545 as protection against French raids. Today the castle is a museum of historical and archaeological interest, exhibiting memorabilia of Portsmouth as a harbour and fortress.

Portsmouth's history and industry has been dominated by its docks. Today it is a thriving commercial port and incorporates shipbuilding, ship-maintenance, electronics and aircraft-engineering industries. As well as being a tourist centre, visitors daily embark on car ferries or hovercraft sailing to Cherbourg, St Malo, the Channel Islands, Le Havre and the Isle of Wight.

Entertainments in the city include special Navy Days held in August.

HMS Victory; and Portsmouth Cathedral.

PORTSMOUTH

Portsmouth is dominated by its docks, where visitors can see a ship figurehead (above, left); the statue of Lord Nelson (above); the Nelson ship (right); and the Britain and Australia band of friendship (below).

MARY ROSE, HMS WARRIOR, VICTORY Portsmouth, Hampshire

Henry VIII established the first major naval base at Portsmouth in 1540. Since that time it has remained the chief Royal Naval seaport and today the Naval Heritage at Portsmouth illustrates that history with three examples of historic warships.

The **Mary Rose**, Henry VIII's famous warship, was recovered in 1982 after resting on the sea bed, a mile off Portsmouth, for over 400 years. Today visitors can view the hull of the ship through a swirling mist of conservation sprays.

In July 1545 the Mary Rose — one of the first purpose-built sailing warships — sailed out of Portsmouth to intercept a French invasion fleet, but before she could open fire she keeled over and both ship and crew were lost.

In the 1960s divers discovered the site and found that the Solent silts had preserved the ship, making it a time capsule of Tudor life at sea. An ambitious project to recover her began in 1979 when the Mary Rose Trust was formed.

The climax of this operation came in October 1982 when the hull was raised to the surface. Visitors can view not only the ship but almost 2,000 artefacts recovered from the sea.

HMS Warrior was launched in 1869 and at that time was the world's largest, fastest and best armed warship.

Visitors can view the four decks which have been restored to appear as they did on their first commission in 1861. Visitors can experience something of the life of the 19th-century Navy by wandering around and examining exhibits which include the cat-o'-nine-tails, and a Colt 45 revolver. A working reproduction of the Penn twin cylinder steam engine is also demonstrated regularly.

Quartermasters dressed in 1860 uniforms are also on hand to answer questions and assist visitors, who can, if they wish, ask to see the Captain.

The **Victory** — Nelson's famous flagship — has been displayed at the base since 1920, when she was brought to dry dock after over 150 years continuous commission. Today as the flagship of Portsmouth she is manned by the Royal Navy and Royal Marines personnel.

One of the Victory's most famous campaigns started in September 1805 when she was boarded by Vice-Admiral Viscount Nelson. Five weeks later Nelson had smashed the Franco Spanish fleet at Trafalgar, but was dead. The Victory returned with Nelson's body in December, and was refitted at Chatham.

Preservation of the vessel continues, and today she is maintained in the configuration she held at the Battle of Trafalgar.

Visitors can see nearly 2,000 artefacts recovered from the sea at the Mary Rose Exhibition.

Part of the Mary Rose (left) which was recovered in 1982, having spent over 400 years on the sea bed a mile off Portsmouth.

ATHELHAMPTON *Dorchester, Dorset*

Built in 1485, the Great Hall of Athelhampton is one of the finest examples of 15th-century domestic architecture. The inhabited mansion – which has enjoyed five centuries of history as a family house – includes some 16th-century additions.

Interesting features include a timbered roof, an oriel window, heraldic glass, secret staircases, a Tudor Great Chamber, and an exquisitely furnished State Bedroom, and an 18th-century dining room.

The house is set in twenty acres of beautiful grounds encircled by the River Piddle. Within the grounds are eight walled gardens containing rare plants, topiary and fountain pools. There are also thatched stables, and a 15th-century dovecote.

Athelhampton retains the happy atmosphere of a private family house, as it has for the past 500 years.

The house is situated one mile east of Puddletown, near Dorchester and is open to the public from Easter to October on Wednesdays, Thursdays, Sundays and bank holidays, and also on Tuesdays in July, August and September.

EXBURY GARDENS
near Southampton, Hampshire

Exbury Gardens were created in the 1920s by Lionel de Rothschild and his son Edmund in 200 acres of natural woodland by the River Beaulieu and the New Forest. Since then the collection of rhododendrons, azaleas, camellias and magnolias have gained worldwide fame. Today the de Rothschild heirs continue to nurture and improve their inheritance.

The gardens were created to give an ever-changing display of beauty and visitors can view a kaleidoscope of colours, including the hardy rhododendrons viewed from the Exbury bridge and evergreen and deciduous azaleas that grow in abundance beside the main drive of Yard Wood.

The gardens are located three miles south east of Beaulieu and are open to the public during spring through to early summer, when azaleas and rhododendrons are in full bloom. The plant centre and gift shop remain open throughout the year.

BEAULIEU Hampshire

Set in the heart of the New Forest, Beaulieu offers visitors not only a chance to view an extensive National Motor Museum, but an opportunity to appreciate the majestic splendour of The Palace House, Gardens and Abbey.

The National Motor Museum comprises of 250 historic cars, commercial vehicles and motor cycles including the 1892 Knight – the earliest petrol driven car of an all British design. Other exhibits include the Pennington – a three wheeler with a top speed of 45mph – which held the land speed record of its time, and Sir Donald Campbell's 'Bluebird'.

The presence of colourful characters from the past such as 'Honest 'Arry Stone' – a well known bombsite car dealer – brings the museum to life.

The admission fee includes entry to the museum, the Palace House, Beaulieu Abbey and a ride on 'Wheels'. This takes visitors in space age pods through a 100 year time tunnel of motoring history from the motor pioneers to the fantasies of the future.

Beaulieu also encapsulates the timeless beauty of an Edwardian stately home. The Palace House – originally the Great Gatehouse to Beaulieu Abbey – has been home to the Montagu family since 1538 and today is one of England's most famous historic homes.

Beaulieu Abbey was founded in 1204 but was largely destroyed under the terms of the Dissolution. Luckily much of the Abbey remains to demonstrate its former beauty. The Domus houses an exhibition of monastic life dating back to the time of King John and the Cistercian Monks, the old refectory is a parish church and the lay dormitory is a restaurant.

Beaulieu's attractions vary from its majestic Palace House and Gardens, to its extensive National Motor Museum.

LONGDOWN FARM
Longdown, Ashurst, Hampshire

Unlike many modern establishments Longdown Farm is home to a wide variety of animals including several breeds of sheep, goats (including some Pygmy goats) and some families of pigs. The farm also has some rare Iron Age pigs which are famous locally as the mascots of Ringwood Breweries.

The poultry shed is frequently full of hatching chicks, duckling and goslings. The farm breeds Chinese geese, Japanese quails, and Silky bantams, as well as the more common domestic poultry. All the poultry are free-range and their eggs can be bought from the farm shop.

The milking shed is a computerised 'herringbone' parlour and visitors can watch cows being milked automatically. This routine is fully automated, from the delivery of the correct amount of feed to the cow's trough to the release of the suction cluster when the udder is emptied.

Visitors are also given the chance to touch the gentler animals. They can stroke new born calves, and cuddle furry rabbits, but are warned that the pigs do bite.

The information units and computer room demonstrate how computers are used in farming, and give information such as what farmers are doing to conserve the environment.

Longdown Farm is open daily from April to October.

MERLEY HOUSE AND MODEL MUSEUM Merley, Wimborne, Dorset

Merley House was built in the 1750s by sugar planter, Ralph Willet, but the most eminent of its owners was William Charles Wentworth who gained self-government for New South Wales, Australia in 1854. The last inhabitants of the house were the Hambro family who left in the 1930s.

Recently Merley House has undergone restoration and one of its most noted features is a wooden staircase made of Lignum Vitae. The house also boasts some of the finest Georgian Plaster Ceilings in the country.

Exhibited in the house is a display of the present owners' collection of some 4000 model toy cars, ships and aeroplanes dating from the 1930s to the present day. These include the land speed record racing cars through the ages and models demonstrating the way cars have developed since the 1890s.

Also on display are some N-Gauge working railways with layouts which include the seventeen foot display by John Wylie – as seen on television – while the working displays include the 100 wagon train of Graham Farish.

At Longdown Farm visitors can touch the gentler animals.

ROMSEY Hampshire

The ancient market town of Romsey provides the New Forest's centre. In the 10th century the town had a great abbey, but today the 12th-century abbey church of St Mary and St Ethelfleda is all that remains of the original.

The church contains many treasures including an illuminated manuscript of the 15th century, a Saxon sculpture depicting the Crucifixion, and an exterior Saxon carving of Christ Crucified. Close to the abbey is King John's hunting lodge which was built in 1210 and has some fine Norman dog-tooth carvings.

Romsey stands on the River Test, which is noted for its trout and salmon. Local industries include beer bottling, jam making, basket-making and tourism, but perhaps the town is better known for the presence of Broadlands, the home of Lord Palmerston and the late Lord Louis Mountbatten of Burma.

Built during the mid-Georgian period the Palladian house stands beside the River Test in a 400-acre park designed by Lancelot 'Capability' Brown. Originally the house belonged to Lord Palmerston – the former prime minister – whose statue graces the market place.

Lord Mountbatten first opened Broadlands to the public in 1979 and present-day visitors can view the elegant 18th-century interior. Indeed many of the original paintings, furniture, porcelain and pieces of sculpture collected by the 2nd Viscount Palmerston still remain.

The William and Mary stable building houses the Mountbatten Exhibition which gives an insight into a naval career spanning six decades. An audiovisual display demonstrates his naval inventions: the daring exploits on the Kelly, the story of his diplomatic success as the last Viceroy of India, the winning of the war in South East Asia and his appointment as First Sea Lord.

The Palladian House, Broadlands, is one of England's most elegant country homes, a striking example of mid-Georgian architecture.

Corfe Castle overlooks the village that takes its name.

CORFE CASTLE *near Wareham, Dorset*

Corfe Castle was created by William I and today is the most impressive ruin in southern England. The castle has had a chequered history. In 978 a hunting lodge on the site was the place King Edward 'The Martyr' was murdered on the orders of his step-mother who wanted the throne for her son Ethelred (the Unready). King John also used the castle as his treasure-house and prison. There was a further twist to the story during the Civil War when the Roundheads failed to enter the castle and a traitorous member of the garrison let them in.

After this battle the castle was condemned, but gunpowder could not completely destroy the sturdy Norman masonry. The great towers although displaced, still stand. Today the castle is a museum exhibiting items of local interest and a model of the old village and castle before its destruction.

The village – which takes the full name of

the castle towering above it – is the centre for the Company of Marblers and Stone-Cutters of the Isle of Purbeck, the oldest trade union in the world.

The castle is open to the public daily from March to October, and weekends from November to February.

PAULTONS PARK
Ower, Romsey, Hampshire

Set in 140 acres of beautiful parkland, Paultons Park has extensive gardens, a lake, a working water mill and over 1000 exotic birds and animals.

Special features of the Park include Kids Kingdom, which is set in three acres of land, and incorporates climbing structures, cable-ways, a tube slide and Spiral Spiderweb. There is also Percy's Bouncer, a mini Ferraris, a miniature railway, a six-lane Astroglide and the Magic Forest where nursery rhymes come to life.

For the more thoughtful the Land of the Dinosaurs recreates a very different Britain, while the Village Life Museum recaptures a more recent, but still harsh, way of life at the beginning of the century. The Romany Museum exhibits fine examples of the highly decorative gypsy wagons and crafts.

The Park is home to tropical birds, parrots, macaws, flamingos, emus, peacocks, owls and over 100 species of wildfowl. Visitors can enjoy walking through the woodlands or along the riverside paths.

The Park is located just off Exit 2 of the M27 near Southampton and is open from early March until early November.

SIR GEORGE STAUNTON
CONSERVATORY Havant, Hampshire

Visitors to Sir George Staunton's Conservatory can experience a tropical rain forest without venturing further than deepest Hampshire.

The conservatory comprises of a tropical rain forest recreated using a collection of plants acquired over many years. It is run by Anmore Exotics, holders of numerous gold medals for displays of tropical and sub-tropical plants awarded by the Royal Horticultural Society. Now rarer species are being propagated to preserve them from extinction.

Enjoy a ride on the six-lane astroglide at Paultons Park.

The conservatory is home to the giant water lily (Victoria Regia.) Sir George Staunton – in whose estate the park is set – was one of the first people to grow the plant in this country. The lily is enormous and, it is claimed, inspired Sir Joseph Paxton – an architect who was initially a gardener – to create the Crystal Palace.

In the Ecology section the symbiotic relationship between plants and animals is illustrated. Tree frogs can be seen hiding in bromeliads, and visitors can view tropical fish and reptiles and insect-eating plants in action.

WINCHESTER Hampshire

Winchester is the capital of Wessex and during Saxon times, as the residence of the Saxon kings, rivalled London as the national capital.

The many historic buildings scattered around the city are evidence of this former supremacy. Winchester Cathedral was built in the 11th century on Saxon foundations and is the longest cathedral in Europe. It contains many royal tombs including that of William Rufus who was killed hunting in the New Forest.

Winchester was once the site of a medieval castle but today The Great Hall is all that remains of the royal residence. Exhibits include the famous Round Table weighing $1\frac{1}{4}$ tons and measuring eighteen feet in diameter which hangs on the west wall.

The Military Museum in Peninsula Barracks exhibits memorabilia from some of the British Army's finest regiments. These include The Royal Hussars, The Light Infantry, The Royal Hampshires, The Ghurkas and The Royal Green Jackets. This collection of military history ranges from 1702 to the present day.

Using modern state-of-the-art technology, visitors to Winchester can now step back into medieval times and join King Richard on the Third Crusade. Within the medieval walls of St John's house, The Crusades

Statue of King Alfred.

Experience recreates the vivid world of courage and pageantry.

Other attractions include the Edwardian Theatre Royal, the River Park Leisure Centre, and Intech, an interactive Technology Exhibition, found in Hampshire Technology Centre.

MID HANTS WATERCRESS LINE

The Mid-Hants Railway – now known as the 'Watercress Line' – can be found seven miles east of Winchester off the A31. The working steam railway is beautifully preserved and runs over a ten mile line from the old cloth-making and brewery town of Alton to Alresford.

During the journey passengers can enjoy the scenic views of some of the most beautiful Hampshire countryside, passing through the famous watercress area and Chawton where Jane Austen completed her six novels.

The train stops at Ropley where passengers can see a variety of steam locomotives in various stages of development.

The railway is open to the public on Sundays only from January to Easter, and on Saturdays, Sundays and bank holidays from Easter to June and September to October. During June to mid July visitors are advised to check the timetable as there are some extra mid-week openings, with daily trains running from mid July to September.

Travel through the beautiful countryside of Hampshire on the Mid Hants Watercress Line.

SALISBURY Wiltshire

There was an Iron Age camp close to Salisbury long before the Romans came to Britain. This camp was strengthened by the Romans and called Serviodunum. In 1075 the Normans arrived and built a castle and cathedral on the site and called it Sarum, but in the 13th century Bishop Herbert Poore decided the site was too small and dismantled the cathedral, building a new one to the south.

Salisbury Cathedral was consecrated in 1258, but the spire, cloisters and chapter house were built later in 1334. The spire rises to 404 feet and is the highest in England.

The cathedral is the resting place for the Earl of Salisbury, who was buried in 1226. He is said to have witnessed the signing of the Magna Carta by his half brother King John and to have brought back the copy – now displayed in the Chapter House – which is one of only four surviving originals.

Salisbury stands at the confluence of the rivers Avon and Nadder. In the 13th century the rivers were bridged and Salisbury became a thriving market and wool centre. Today there is still a twice weekly market held in the market square. Salisbury reached the peak of its prosperity in the 18th century and it is during this period that many of the houses in the cathedral close were built. Today some of them house the many museums of the area.

Opposite the west door of the cathedral is the King's House which is now the Salisbury and South Wiltshire Museum. Exhibits include galleries of Stonehenge, Early Man, Old Sarum, Salisbury and the Giant.

Close by, the Bishop's Wardrobe is home to the Museum of the Duke of Edinburgh's Royal Regiment. Here 200 years of the Regiment's history is on display.

One of the finest 18th-century houses in the close is Mompesson House which was

The spire of Salisbury Cathedral is the tallest in England.

built for Charles Mompesson in 1701. For the past 100 years the house has been home to the Townsend family.

To the north of Salisbury is Salisbury Plain where thousands of troops have been stationed, among them 33,000 Canadians who camped out in the bitter winter of 1914–15.

NEW FOREST MUSEUM AND VISITOR CENTRE
Lyndhurst, Hampshire

The New Forest was a favourite haunt of William the Conquerer who named it 'Nova Foresta' and for centuries the forest was the hunting ground of English kings. Over 900 years later the ancient forest and heathland – which is still subject to laws created by William to protect the red deer – remains for visitors to enjoy.

Although renowned for the famous wild ponies the forest is home to many more plants and animals that are often never seen. Today visitors to the New Forest Museum and Visitor Centre at Lyndhurst can see that hidden forest.

The visit begins with 'The Changing Forest', a multi-projector audiovisual show of hundreds of colour photographs of the forest through the four seasons. Also in the exhibition are some artefacts – mostly life-sized models and displays – which tell the story of 'Brusher' Mills, a famous New Forest Snakecatcher. The centre also includes computer data banks and quiz sheets for children.

DENMEAD POTTERY
Denmead, near Waterlooville, Hampshire

Denmead Pottery is one of Hampshire's most modern commercial potteries, and produces over 3,000 units of pottery a day. Each day visitors are welcome to tour the factory and view the entire production process of a traditional craft that was first conceived in Japan in 10,000 BC.

A visit to the pottery would not be complete without a trip to the factory shop which is open daily and where visitors can buy genuine factory seconds.

Set in twenty acres of landscaped grounds with an ornamental lake the pottery is the ideal location for a day trip. The grounds are surrounded by 300 acres of woodlands where there are picnic areas. There is also an adventure play area and pets corner for children.

ISLE OF WIGHT

Separated from the mainland of southern England by the Solent and Spithead, the Isle of Wight has a 60-mile coastal perimeter. This provides excellent facilities for keen yachtsmen and fishermen. Cowes is the yachting capital and each year hosts the Cowes Regatta.

Local industry includes agriculture, shipbuilding and tourism. The Isle of Wight is popular for its sandy beaches, deep coastal ravines, grottos and rock formations, in particular the Needles, and there are many attractions for visitors.

A popular attraction is the steam railway running from Haven Street to Wootton. Visitors can see a unique collection of

The Old Village, Shanklin, Isle of Wight.

The Coloured Cliffs, Alum Bay.

locomotives and rolling stock, some over 120 years old. They can also ride on locomotives which take them either in the splendour of Victorian first class accommodation, or the more functional Edwardian wooden panelled carriages.

Situated on the south western coast of the Isle lies Blackgang Chine, a deep rocky cleft in a shore which has claimed 180 ships since 1750. Set 400 feet above Chale Bay is the Blackgang Chine Fantasy Theme Park.

The park was opened in 1842 by Alexander Dabell and has been developed by succeeding generations of the family. Today it incorporates Aviaries, Nursery Land, Jungleland, Smugglers Lugger, an Indian Village and a Victorian water-powered sawmill.

Other places of interest include the Museum of the History of Smuggling (at Wroxall), which illustrates over 700 years of the profession, the Museum of the Isle of Wight Geology – which exhibits over 5000 fossils found on the island – Flamingo Park at Seaview, a Lilliput Doll and Toy Museum, and Osborn-Smith's Wax Museum and Animal World situated at Sandown. Other places of interest are Barton Manor Vineyard Gardens at East Cowes, Butterfly and Fountain World at Wootton, the Roman Villa and the world famous wax museum at Brading, the Needles Pleasure Park and the Isle of Wight Zoo at Sandown.

For Further Information Contact:

Tourist Information Centre
Above Bar Precinct
SOUTHAMPTON
Hampshire SO9 4XF
Telephone: (0703) 221106

Tourist Information Centre
The Guildhall
The Broadway
WINCHESTER
Hampshire SO23 9LJ
Telephone: (0962) 67871

Southern Tourist Board
40 Chamberlayne Road
EASTLEIGH
Hampshire SO5 5JH
Telephone: (0703) 616027

THAMES AND CHILTERNS

Oxford Canal

Although the Thames and Chilterns teem with bustling market towns, once off the beaten track, the countryside is both tranquil and beautiful. In Bedfordshire there is the large open space of Dunstable Downs, dotted with country parks, nature reserves, and estates that are open to the public.

The Chilterns run through Buckinghamshire and are all that remain of the vast beechwood forest that once stretched across Britain. In the heart of Buckinghamshire lies the Vale of Aylesbury, an area of flat, mostly dairy, farmland which is sharply contrasted by sudden hills such as Brill Hill at Quainton and Lodge Hill at Waddesdon.

For centuries Hertfordshire has been an agricultural area producing mostly wheat and barley, while Oxfordshire farms are chiefly arable. Industry in Oxfordshire is centred around Cowley, while Oxford — the administrative centre — is noted for its church spires, and has been a city of learning since the 13th century.

Berkshire is one of the smallest and most beautiful shire counties in England and incorporates the royal town of Windsor and the race course at Ascot where the first race meeting was held over 270 years ago.

All these counties are interlaced by canals once used for the transportation of goods. Latterly much has been done to re-open these, and many are now navigable for tourist trips around these historic counties.

The area's eventful past pervades its present aspect in many varied ways. Buildings are the most obvious witness to the past. The historic house of Shaw's Corner at Ayot St Lawrence was the home of George Bernard Shaw. Milton moved to Chalfont St Giles to escape the plague of London, and the cottage where he lived has been open to the public ever since. Blenheim Palace — the home of the first Duke of Marlborough — is perhaps better known as the birthplace of Sir Winston Churchill.

The area has several vineyards selling a variety of fruit wines including elderflower wine and gooseberry champagne. Many of the pubs also serve traditional beer, and Charrington's has over 400 pubs in the area.

THAMES & CHILTERNS

BEDFORD

A428

Great Ouse

BEDFORDSHIRE

MILTON KEYNES

A34

A41

1   M1

A120

OXFORDSHIRE

A40   12   2

LUTON   A1   A10

3

7

AYLESBURY   HERTFORDSHIRE

OXFORD   9   ST ALBANS

A420   M40

M25   13

Thames

11   HIGH WYCOMBE   10

4

14   15   BUCKINGHAMSHIRE

HENLEY   6

BERKSHIRE   8   SLOUGH

M4   WINDSOR

READING

5   A4

1	Woburn Abbey
2	Blenheim Palace
3	Luton Hoo
4	Bekonscot Model Village
5	Littlecote House
6	Courage Shire Horse Centre
7	Cotswold Woollen Weavers
8	Beale Bird Park
9	Mill Green Museum and Watermill
10	John Milton's Cottage
11	Didcot Railway Centre
12	Cogges Manor Farm Museum
13	Capel Manor Horticultural & Environmental Centre
14	Wayland's Smithy
15	Uffington Castle

BLENHEIM PALACE
Woodstock, Oxfordshire

In recognition of his victory over the French at Blenheim in 1704, John Churchill, 1st Duke of Marlborough, had the mansion which bears the battle-site's name built for him. A gift from Queen Anne, England's largest country house was designed by Sir John Vanbrugh, is now the home of the 11th Duke, and was the birthplace of one of the country's greatest statesmen, Sir Winston Churchill.

Vanbrugh's Baroque masterpiece houses tapestries, paintings, sculpture and fine furniture in magnificent state rooms. Especially beautiful is the Long Library, containing over 10,000 volumes. On display too is the room where Winston Churchill was born, as well as some of his paintings, personal belongings, letters, books and photographs.

Blenheim's 2000-acre gardens were landscaped in the late 18th century by Capability Brown. Among their present day attractions is the Garden Centre with its Butterfly House, where tropical butterflies and moths live in the nearest thing possible to their natural environment, and an adventure play area.

Hour-long tours of the palace start at regular intervals every day from mid-March to the end of October, though visitors are welcome to explore it independently. The Butterfly House, too, is open from mid-March to the end of October, and the Park all year round (except Christmas Day).

Blenheim Palace (below), designed by Vanbrugh with gardens landscaped by Capability Brown. The room at Blenheim (above) where Winston Churchill was born.

BEKONSCOT MODEL VILLAGE
Beaconsfield, Buckinghamshire

Now in its 61st year, the model village of Bekonscot grew out of a London accountant's hobby in the 1920s. Its miniature world captures the atmosphere of rural England in the 1930s, complete with a cricket match never interrupted by rain or bad light and 500 yards of 1-gauge model railway track with seven stations. During the open season between March and October, the railway's 22 locomotives – along with their coaches and goods wagons – make journeys totalling a staggering 4,200 miles.

Bekonscot's 1,200 hand-carved inhabitants have their own zoo, cinema, minster, flying club, fishing village and lake. Set in 1½ acres, the village also offers full-size refreshment facilities, picnic sites and play areas for visitors.

LITTLECOTE HOUSE
Hungerford, Berkshire

Two miles west of Hungerford, the Tudor estate where Littlecote House stands has been transformed into an award-winning attraction where visitors can see history come to life.

The gabled Elizabethan mansion contains a unique collection of Cromwellian armour. Lifelike wax figures and an audio commentary re-create the day when a colonel in the 17th-century English Civil War sent his wife away to safety before fighting broke out, and there are guides to answer visitors' questions.

In the grounds, there are daily exhibitions of jousting and falconry, a re-created 17th-century village, a rare-breeds farm and craft village. A little steam railway carries visitors to the site where a Roman villa is being excavated, and to Fort Littlecote, a giant adventure playground for children.

Regular special events are held at week-

The miniature world of Bekonscot has been attracting visitors for over 60 years.

ends throughout Littlecote's open season, which runs from early April until the end of September. They range from historical spectaculars to rallies for classic-vehicle enthusiasts.

LUTON HOO *Luton, Bedfordshire*

Although there have been substantial dwellings on the same site since the 13th century, and possibly even earlier, the present house at Luton Hoo was originally built by architect Robert Adam in 1767. Rebuilt after a disastrous fire in 1843, it was bought by Sir Julius Wernher, one of the pioneers of the diamond industry in South Africa, in 1903.

It was Sir Julius who laid the foundations of the matchless Wernher Collection, including superb paintings, tapestries, furniture, medieval ivories, Renaissance jewellery and porcelain, which is one of the property's major attractions. Later additions were brought to Luton Hoo by the late Lady Zia Wernher, great-granddaughter of Emperor

Luton Hoo.

Nicholas I of Russia, who married Sir Julius's son Harold. Her inheritance included a unique collection of Russian Fabergé jewellery, as well as mementoes of the Russian Imperial family.

Luton Hoo's 4000-acre grounds still bear the stamp of Capability Brown's landscaping in the mid-18th century, though the formal gardens around the house were created at the turn of the 20th century by Romayne Walker.

Now in the hands of Nicholas Phillips, grandson of Sir Harold and Lady Zia, the house at Luton Hoo is open between mid-April and mid-October (afternoons only; closed Mondays apart from bank holidays),

and the gardens – like the house, closed on Mondays except for bank holidays – open all year round.

COGGES MANOR FARM MUSEUM
Witney, Oxfordshire

On the outskirts of Witney is a nineteen-acre farm museum run by Oxfordshire's Department of Leisure and Arts. Its manor house has been restored to show how life was lived there 80 years ago, when it was the centre of a thriving farm: inside it, and in the farm buildings that surround it, Edwardian agricultural life has been re-created. Within the farm, and in the fields nearby, are some of the animals on which the farm depended.

Regular demonstrations of country skills and crafts – blacksmithing, hurdle making, sheep shearing, butter churning, hand milking and farmhouse cooking – take place throughout the summer season, which runs from April to November (closed on Mondays apart from bank holidays, and on Sunday mornings). There is a daily programme of activities in and around the farm, showing the kind of chores that had to be done to care for both the animals and the people who looked after them.

Nature and history trails are laid out so that visitors can explore the grounds and village in which the farm is set.

COTSWOLD WOOLLEN WEAVERS
Near Lechlade, Oxfordshire

Five hundred years ago, great flocks of sheep roamed the Cotswolds. There are fewer today, but in the village of Filkins, between Burford and Lechlade, some of the history associated with them lives on.

In one of the 18th-century barns which marked the transition from sheep-rearing to arable farming in the area, Cotswold Woollen Weavers use traditional skills and machinery to manufacture a wide range of cloth, garments, knitwear, rugs and accessories.

Visitors are welcome to tour the working weaving mill all year round, any day of the week (closed Sunday mornings). An exhibition gallery illustrates the history of wool in the Cotswolds, and tells the story of how wool becomes cloth; the end results of the weavers' handiwork are on sale at the mill shop. Refreshments are available, and there is a picnic area too.

MILL GREEN MUSEUM AND WATERMILL Hatfield, Hertfordshire

Housed in what used to be the home of the millers who worked the mill next door, Mill Green Museum has two permanent galleries displaying local items from Roman times to the present day – everything from pottery and craft tools to underwear and school certificates. Temporary exhibitions are mounted in the third gallery, and publicised locally in advance. Special craft displays and demonstrations take place here on most weekends throughout the summer.

Adjoining the museum is the watermill, which has been restored into full working order by the Hatfield and District Archaeological Society. Extensive renovation included repairs to the building's fabric, the installation of a new staircase, renovation of the mill machinery, and the construction of a new water wheel – all of which now means that, after an interval of 75 years when the mill was in a state of disrepair, flour can again be ground here.

Both museum and watermill are open throughout the year, on Tuesdays to Fridays all day, and afternoons on Saturdays, Sundays and bank holidays. Milling normally takes place on Tuesdays, Wednesdays and Sunday afternoons.

JOHN MILTON'S COTTAGE
Chalfont St Giles, Buckinghamshire

Poet John Milton came to Chalfont St Giles to escape the plague in 1665. Old and blind, he completed the epic *Paradise Lost* here, and wrote *Paradise Regained.* His 16th-century cottage was bought by the village people in 1887 and has been open to the public ever since. The house with its collections of Milton memorabilia, the library containing early editions of his work, and a beautifully maintained cottage garden can be visited every day except Mondays between early March and the end of October (open bank holiday Mondays).

Also worth seeing in Chalfont St Giles is the Chalfont Shire Horse Centre (open daily, April to September) and the Chiltern Open Air Museum, whose old buildings and bygones help re-create the history of the area. Regular displays of rural arts and crafts are held here during the open season, which runs from April to October (opening days vary).

The 16th-century cottage (opposite page) where John Milton wrote Paradise Lost *has been open to the public since 1887.*

Mill Green Watermill, a fully restored 18th-century water-powered corn mill, adjoins a local history museum in the home of the millers.

WINDSOR Berkshire

Windsor has been the home and burial place of England's monarchs for 900 years. William the Conqueror began its fine castle, still a favourite royal residence, envisaging it as one of a ring of fortresses that would defend London, but it was Henry I who first lived and held court there early in the 12th century.

Later monarchs left their mark on Windsor Castle in the shape of extended stone defences (Henry II) and D-shaped towers (Henry III). Elizabeth I had many of its ancient wooden buildings cleared and replaced, and Edward IV began St George's Chapel where Henry VIII now shares a tomb with Jane Seymour, his favourite wife.

Modernised in the French style under Charles II (1660–85), but neglected by George I and II, Windsor's status as a royal

The River Thames (left); St George's Chapel, Windsor Castle (below).

Windsor

Royal Windsor, overlooked by the castle (above), lies in the charming rural countryside of Berkshire, and offers plenty for the visitor to do and see.

residence was restored by George III. It was his son who began the Waterloo Chamber to celebrate the famous English victory in 1815, and George IV was the last ruler to make significant changes. His alterations affected the whole outline of the castle, and it still looks much as it did in his day.

Windsor Castle and its precincts are open to the public all year, though the magnificent State Apartments are closed when HM The Queen is in official residence.

The town of Windsor has two museums: one devoted to its history is housed in Sir Christopher Wren's 17th-century Guildhall, not far from the castle; the other, in Combermere Barracks, displays the uniforms and arms of the Household Cavalry regiments.

Several pleasure-boat operators run trips along the stretch of the Thames that flows through Windsor, and the river is an excellent vantage-point from which to see the town. Windsor Bridge, built of cast iron in 1821, crosses it and leads to one of Britain's most famous schools, Eton College.

A working farm is the home of the Courage prize-winning Shire horses.

COURAGE SHIRE HORSE CENTRE
Maidenhead, Berkshire

The home of Courage brewery's prize-winning Shire horses is a working farm just outside Maidenhead. It is open to the public every day between the beginning of March and the end of October.

Up to twelve of the beautiful Shires, each weighing in at around a ton, are in residence at any one time. On display with them are the brilliantly-polished harnesses and brasses that are their exhibition finery, and some of the rosettes and trophies they have won at shows all over the country.

An audiovisual presentation tells the history of the breed, and conveys some of the excitement they feel when they are being prepared for a show. 'Live' attractions include the chance to see a farrier, wheelwright or cooper at work; free guided tours are run throughout the day.

Refreshments and souvenirs are on sale, and there is an adventure playground for children.

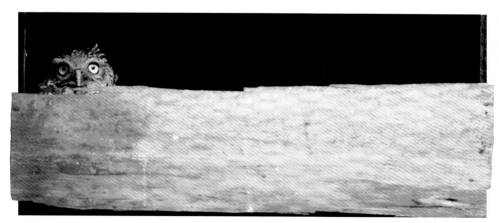

An owl at Beale Bird Park looks suspiciously from its nest.

BEALE BIRD PARK
Lower Basildon, Berkshire

On a fifteen-acre Thames-side site, Beale Bird Park has grown from a small pond, a dirt road and a few peacocks into a nature reserve and leisure facility complete with children's play areas, picnic sites and education centre.

Created in 1956, the Child-Beale Wildlife Trust which maintains the Park has been responsible for introducing ornamental waterfowl and many other birds from flamingoes to owls. Rare breeds of birds and

livestock are bred here as part of the Trust's conservation work. The Trust's policy of active environmental protection has encouraged many wild British birds, animals and flowers to make their home here.

Though the welfare of the site's wildlife is the Trust's primary concern, another has been to make it accessible to the public. Facilities for visitors include scenic picnic areas overlooking ornamental statues and fountains, an adventure playground, and a 7¼-inch-gauge model railway giving rides around the site. Guided tours and illustrated talks can be arranged, and the Park's resident education officer is usually on hand to answer questions. Most of the exhibits are along specially created walkways, and close up observation is possible at the pets' corner and Tropical House.

Beale Bird Park is open seven days a week from early March until December, and can be reached by river as well as road and rail.

WAYLAND'S SMITHY and UFFINGTON CASTLE Oxfordshire

Three miles south-west of Uffington is the village of Ashbury and Wayland's Smithy, a 5000-year-old burial place. It seems to have been constructed in two phases: a mummy-shaped mound over an earlier wooden chamber. The whole thing is centred in an oval ring of beeches and surrounded by sarsen stones. Saxon legend, from where its name comes, says a mythological black-

Peacocks were the first birds to be introduced at Beale Bird Park (far left).

smith called Weland is associated with the site: the story goes that if a traveller ties his horse near the entrance, the gods' own smith will shoe it provided that a coin for him is left on the lintel.

On top of a chalk escarpment to the east, over 800 feet above sea level, is Uffington Castle, an ancient hill fort. Covering nearly eight acres, the site has been largely undisturbed over the years, and its beautiful views have made it a popular picnic spot since Victorian times.

Etched in the hillside below the fort is the spectacular equine figure, the oldest of England's seventeen chalk horses, that gives White Horse Hill its name. Its massive outlines are made up of trenches ten feet across and two to three feet deep, and stretch across the turf for 365 feet. Its origins are a mystery, though it is thought to have been there for close on 2000 years.

CAPEL MANOR HORTICULTURAL AND ENVIRONMENTAL CENTRE
Enfield, Middlesex

Set in the grounds of the beautiful Capel Estate are acres of ornamental and experimental gardens. Many small gardens have been created here, each with its own character and charm. Water features and period gardens rub shoulders with gardens specially created for the disabled to enjoy, where the senses of hearing, touch and smell are catered for as well as that of sight.

Seed and plant trials, run in association with *Gardening from Which?*, as well as practical tests of garden implements and buildings, are carried out at Capel Manor, and the centre also offers a full range of horticultural courses for those wishing to pursue specialist interests.

Visitors are welcome between October and March (weekdays only), and April to September (daily). Special events are scheduled for weekends during the summer months.

Not far away is Capel Manor Farm, designed and stocked to help visitors understand more about farming at its best. The Farm is open during weekend afternoons from Easter to October, and every day during the school holidays. Throughout the year, Capel Manor's Environmental Centre offers visitors the chance to take part in a range of educational activities based around countryside and agricultural themes.

DIDCOT RAILWAY CENTRE
Didcot, Oxfordshire

Just 150 years ago, the first trains ran along Isambard Kingdom Brunel's Great Western Railway through Didcot on their way from London to Bristol. Though the GWR no longer exists, it is still affectionately remembered – not least by the members of the Great Western Society who have created the Didcot Railway Centre.

Here, alongside the main line, is a large collection of former GWR locomotives, coaches and rolling-stock of all kinds. Lovingly restored, they form the centrepiece of this working museum, where the original engine shed, coaling stage, turntable and lifting-shop are also on view. A typical country station, complete with signal box, has been re-created to show how it might have looked in the GWR's heyday.

Didcot Railway Centre is open Tuesdays to Sundays and bank holiday Mondays

The golden age of the Great Western Railway is being recreated at Didcot Railway Centre (opposite page).

The grounds of Capel Manor are divided into many smaller gardens which offer changing interest throughout the year.

between April and September, and on weekends only between October and March. Regular special events are held here throughout the year: Steamdays, for example, offer visitors the chance to ride steam trains and see all the normal maintenance activities that used to keep the locomotives running.

WOBURN ABBEY and WOBURN WILD ANIMAL KINGDOM SAFARI PARK Bedfordshire

Woburn Abbey, home of the Dukes of Bedford for over 300 years, is set in a magnificent 3000-acre deer park landscaped by Humphry Repton in the 19th century. Nine species of deer live here, one of which – the Milu, or Pere David breed – was actually preserved from extinction by Woburn, which is now home to the largest breeding herd in the world.

Rebuilt in the 18th century, and later extensively altered by the Prince Regent's architect, Henry Holland, Woburn Abbey is one of Britain's most famous stately homes. It contains the superb State apartments where the newly married Victoria and Albert once slept in the four-poster State bed, and a magnificent art collection includes works by Gainsborough, Rembrandt, Reynolds and Van Dyck. Private collections of furniture, porcelain and silver are also on display.

Woburn Abbey is open at weekends only in spring, then every day from early April to late October. Visitors can view its private apartments when they are not being used by the family. Various special exhibitions and events are held in the Abbey's grounds throughout the summer season.

Britain's largest drive-through safari park is about a mile from Woburn Abbey. Tigers, lions, rhinos, hippos, giraffes, monkeys, camels and Canadian timber wolves are just some of the species that roam here. Special attractions include displays by sea-lions and parrots as well as working elephants, and a pets' corner. The Safari Park is open daily from mid-March to October.

Woburn Wild Animal Kingdom is Britain's largest drive-through safari park.

OXFORD Oxfordshire

Home of one of the world's most famous universities, Oxford's history as a seat of learning goes back as far as the 12th century. Its central square mile alone has over 600 buildings listed as architecturally and historically important: among its finest are said to be All Soul's College (founded 1437), Christ Church (1525), Magdalen (1458), Merton (1264) and Queen's (established in the 14th century).

Most of the colleges open their quadrangles and chapels to afternoon visitors, and full details of opening times can be found in *Welcome to Oxford*, available from the Tourist Information Centre.

Over the centuries, Oxford University and its colleges have amassed formidable collections of works of art and antiquities. Some of the best are to be found in the Ashmolean Museum (famous for its antiquities from the Near East, Greece and Rome, as well as European paintings and stringed instru-

ments); the Museum of the History of Science, whose exhibits include Europe's largest collections of astrolabes and sundials; the University Museum (natural history); and the Bate Collection of Historical Instruments.

Works by the greatest European Old Masters can be found in Christ Church Picture Gallery, while the Museum of Modern Art brings the picture right up to date with exhibitions of international contemporary painting, drawing, sculpture, photography, film, design and architecture.

Oxford venues play host, too, to the performing arts. The Apollo Theatre is second home to the Welsh National Opera and the Glyndebourne Touring Company, and also stages ballet, pantomime and concerts. During the summer, the City of Oxford Orchestra sponsors a series of concerts in college chapels, the Wren-designed Sheldonian Theatre, and the Holywell Music Room (Europe's oldest concert hall); international

Oxford's Botanic Gardens are overlooked by Magdalen College.

performers visit all year round. Favourite annual events include the 'Handel in Oxford' festival (July) and the spectacular Grand Fireworks concerts (June and July).

The rivers Thames and Cherwell flow through the city, the Cherwell through lush water meadows and near some of the area's most scenic footpaths. Trials for the annual Boat Race against Cambridge are held on the Thames, as are 'bump' races – Torpids in February and Eights Week in May. Punts are for hire, and by tradition glide through the water stern-first – unlike at Cambridge, where the bow leads – and trips on pleasure steamers can be arranged at local boatyards.

Probably the best way to explore Oxford is on foot. Guided two-hour walking tours leave regularly from the Tourist Information Centre, while independent pedestrians can follow a comprehensive route mapped out in *Welcome to Oxford* which takes in many of the city's most attractive sights – including the Botanic Garden, the Frank Cooper Shop and Museum of Marmalade, and Oxford's covered market. There are plenty of bustling pubs *en route*, so refreshment stops are never far away.

Open-topped double-decker buses run circular tours from the railway station and eleven points around the city every day of the year.

Oxford's streets document many periods of English history.

The Radcliffe Camera (below) is the earliest example in England of a round reading room.

For Further Information Contact:

Tourist Information Centre
St Aldates
OXFORD
Oxfordshire OX1 1DY
Telephone: (0865) 726873/726874

Tourist Information Centre
Central Station
Thames Street
WINDSOR
Berkshire SL4 1QU
Telephone: (0753) 854800

Thames & Chilterns Tourist Board
The Mount House
WITNEY
Oxfordshire OX5 6DZ
Telephone: (0993) 778800

SOUTH EAST

Oasthouses are prevalent throughout the south east.

Kent is known as the 'garden of England', because it is largely a fruit and hop growing county. The countryside is scattered with oast-houses, hop gardens, orchards and farms. This landscape gradually becomes more varied as it stretches into the neighbouring counties of East Sussex which produces cereals, hops and vege- tables and West Sussex where crops consist mostly of cereals, root crops and dairy produce.

The rural landscape is one of rolling hills in the downs and the high weald, with winding country lanes and fertile farming lands in the vale of Kent. On the coast there are the legen- dary white cliffs of Dover and the reclaimed marshland of Romney Marsh – once the haunt of smugglers – but now largely sheep grazing land although recently tulips have been intro- duced. Near Tunbridge Wells is Bewl Water – the largest stretch of inland water in the south east of England and Tunbridge Wells itself, which since the early 17th century has been popular for its medi- cinal waters.

The close proximity to the capital has drawn many famous people to the area and relics of these are the many expansive stately homes. Hever Castle, near Eden- bridge was the childhood home of Anne Boleyn; Leeds Castle at Maidstone was converted into a Royal Palace by Henry VIII and was the favourite home of many medieval queens, and the Royal Pavilion at Brighton was created by the Prince Regent who later became George IV.

History has also been made in the county. In 1170 Thomas Becket was martyred in Canterbury Cathedral. Indeed the area has over a hundred museums. These include the Tyrwhitt-Drake Museum of Carriages at Maidstone which houses England's finest collection of horse-drawn vehicles.

Moreover history is still in the making in the area. In 1993 the channel tunnel will open, and visitors wishing for a preview to this momentous occasion should visit the Eurotunnel Exhibition at Folkestone.

The land is fertile and rich in natural food such as Kentish fruit, sea food such as Whitstable Oysters, Romney Marsh lambs, and fruit wines, meads and locally-made beer.

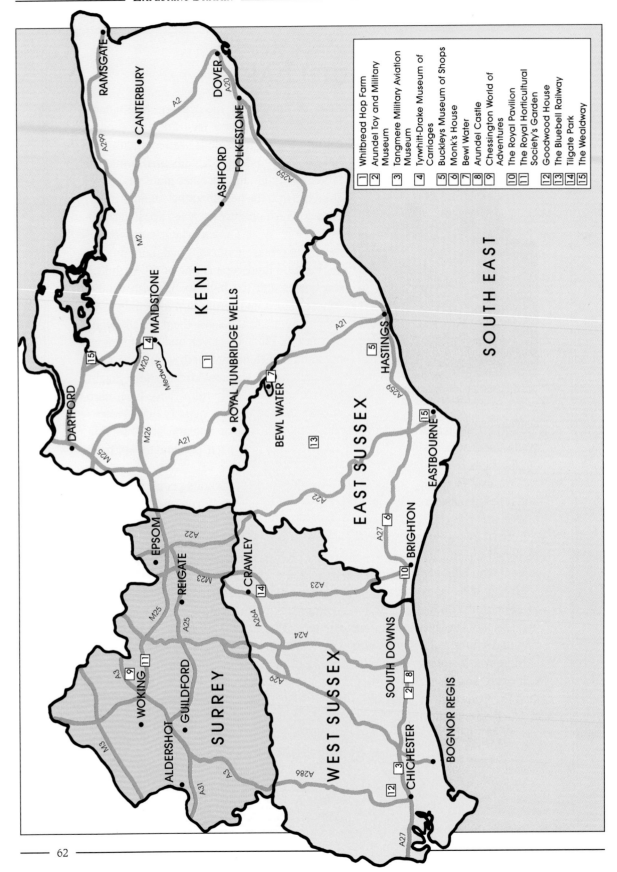

SOUTH EAST

1 Whitbread Hop Farm
2 Arundel Toy and Military Museum
3 Tangmere Military Aviation Museum
4 Tyrwhitt-Drake Museum of Carriages
5 Buckleys Museum of Shops
6 Monk's House
7 Bewl Water
8 Arundel Castle
9 Chessington World of Adventures
10 The Royal Pavilion
11 The Royal Horticultural Society's Garden
12 Goodwood House
13 The Bluebell Railway
14 Tilgate Park
15 The Wealdway

RAMSGATE
CANTERBURY
DOVER
FOLKESTONE
ASHFORD
A299
A2
A20
A259
M2
M20
Medway
MAIDSTONE
KENT
ROYAL TUNBRIDGE WELLS
DARTFORD
M26
M25
A21
A21
BEWL WATER
HASTINGS
A259
EAST SUSSEX
A22
EASTBOURNE
BRIGHTON
A27
A23
EPSOM
A22
REIGATE
CRAWLEY
M23
M25
A25
A26A
A24
A29
SOUTH DOWNS
WOKING
A3
GUILDFORD
SURREY
ALDERSHOT
M3
A3
A31
WEST SUSSEX
A286
CHICHESTER
BOGNOR REGIS
A27

CHESSINGTON WORLD
OF ADVENTURES Chessington, Surrey

Thrilling rides, a spectacular circus and a zoo are on the menu at Chessington·World of Adventures, one of Britain's top theme parks.

Rides include voyages of discovery on the Dragon River and aboard the Smugglers' Galleon on the high seas. A runaway mine train careers through Calamity Canyon, and the Safari Skyway Monorail offers panoramic views of the new zoo area. One of the newest rides is the Vampire, which travels the world's first hanging roller-coaster – soaring above treetop height and plunging below ground.

International circus artistes, clowns, jugglers and acrobats bring their unique skills to the Big Top, and younger children can enjoy their own supervised circus adventure area.

Chessington's zoo has long been a pioneer in developing new ways of keeping animals, birds and reptiles in conditions which allow them maximum freedom without threatening the safety of visitors. It is open every day,

Visitors rush through Calamity Canyon on the Runaway Mine Train.

though closing times vary with the season, while the theme park and circus can be visited between late March and the end of October.

Voyages of Discovery are a main attraction at Chessington World of Adventures.

ARUNDEL CASTLE
Arundel, West Sussex

Restored over the years so that it now appears much as it must have done in medieval days, though its oldest parts actually date back to Norman times, Arundel Castle is situated in magnificent grounds overlooking the River Arun. For over 700 years it has been the seat of the dukes of Norfolk and their ancestors, premier peers and hereditary Earls Marshal of England.

Besieged, bombarded and occupied by Parliamentary forces during the 17th-century Civil War, it was rescued from dilapidation over the next two centuries and rebuilt in superb style. Among its architectural treasures is the splendid Baron's Hall, an 11th-century Keep, and a great deal of fine carving in the Early English Gothic style.

Period furniture and furnishings are on display throughout the castle, some dating from the 16th century. One sumptuous room contains the bed and matching furniture specially made for Queen Victoria and Prince Albert's visit to the castle in 1846.

A rich collection of art treasures includes works by Reynolds, Gainsborough and Van Dyck. Portraits of members of the family, and many reminders of their importance and influence, are on show.

Open to the public at advertised times (except on Saturdays) from late March to the end of October, Arundel Castle also hosts the annual Arundel Festival in late August when its American Ground is the stage for open-air theatre.

The magnificent Arundel Castle (opposite page).

BEWL WATER
Lamberhurst, near Tunbridge Wells, Kent

Part of Southern Water's network of reservoirs, Bewl Water is also a place where visitors can walk, picnic, fish, enjoy wildlife and take part in a variety of water sports in the beautiful High Weald countryside.

Footpaths and riding tracks surround the reservoir, and there is a children's adventure playground. Car-parking and picnic areas are plentiful, and various information sheets available at the Visitor Centre introduce the area's amenities. Craft exhibitions, morris

Water sports at Bewl Water.

dancing and other displays are held on most summer weekends; from April to October, it is possible to take a boat trip on the reservoir itself.

Bewl Water is the premier trout fishery in southern England. Season or day permits for fly-fishing and boat hire are available from the Fishing Lodge between April and October.

Board sailors with their own equipment and a recognised certificate of competence can buy day permits (weekdays only, except bank holidays), and beginners can learn by taking a course here. Organised groups of canoeists are welcome, provided they have their own craft and a qualified instructor; other water-based activities and special events – involving dinghy and board sailing, rowing and sub-aqua diving – are organised throughout the year by various specialist clubs.

Many species of waterfowl and animals make their home around Bewl Water, and 127 acres have been set aside as a nature reserve accessible only to people conducting scientific investigations. Though this site is

Bewl Water's attractions include walking, fishing, wildlife and places to picnic as well as a variety of water sports.

not open to the public, there is a hide on the edge of the reserve for ornithologists, and visitors can still enjoy spotting the many birds, animals and plants visible from walks along the public footpaths around the reservoir.

Goodwood House West Sussex

Home of the Dukes of Richmond, Goodwood House is also a treasure-house of superb paintings, French and English period furniture, tapestries and Sèvres porcelain. Family mementoes with royal connections from the time of Mary, Queen of Scots to the present day are on display, including Queen Victoria's Fabergé walking stick and her Coronation Cushion.

The house, built at the end of the 18th century, is a fine example of Sussex flintwork and surrounded by beautiful parkland. In the grounds is The Shell House, built in 1739 for Sarah, Duchess of Richmond. This small pavilion set on a hill is entirely covered with shells arranged in intricate patterns.

Both house and gardens are open to the public on selected days throughout the summer months. Important equestrian events take place from time to time in the International Dressage Centre in the park. Cream teas are served in the State Supper Rooms on most open days.

The Card Room, Goodwood House.

Nearby Goodwood Racecourse was first used in 1801 and is now one of England's premier horse-racing venues. The land on which it stands was once part of the Goodwood estate.

Every July, Goodwood House was home to tsars, kings and queens who had come for the horseracing.

CANTERBURY Kent

Even before medieval times, Canterbury was a renowned religious centre. Its cathedral, founded in 597 but rebuilt after a fire in 1070, is still mother church for Anglicans all over the world, and dominates the city's skyline. Magnificent architecture, fine medieval stained glass, intricate carvings and ancient paintings make it as popular a destination for pilgrims today as it has been for the centuries since Thomas Becket, then Archbishop of Canterbury, was murdered there almost a thousand years ago.

Still-visible architectural reminders of Canterbury's history go back a very long way: Roman bricks have been found in the walls of St Martin's, said to be the oldest parish church in England. The Normans, too, left their mark in the shape of the castle's Keep and the Norman staircase at the King's School; St John the Baptist's Hospital, the oldest surviving almshouse in England, also dates from this period. The now-restored Weaver's Houses, in typical black and white Tudor style, were once the homes of Flemish and Huguenot refugees from religious persecution.

The 14th-century Poor Priests' Hospital, Stour Street, is now a museum featuring treasures from Canterbury's past. These include items found during excavations in the Roman, Saxon and medieval town. Guided tours re-creating the early Thomas Becket pilgrimages from London to Canterbury are set in the Pilgrims Way Centre, St Margaret's Street, and include audiovisual displays from selected stories of Chaucer's *Canterbury Tales.*

Canterbury Cathedral.

Present-day pilgrims can enjoy a variety of amenities. The Dane John Gardens were originally laid out in 1790, and include a walk along part of the city's medieval walls. Another garden surrounds the impressive ruins of St Augustine's Abbey. There are excellent shopping facilities in the Marlowe Arcade — named, like the new 1000-seat theatre in The Friars, after the pre-Shakespearean playwright Christopher Marlowe who was born in Canterbury. The city has its own sports centre, as well as an indoor swimming pool and facilities for tennis, speedway and greyhound racing.

Annual events include a cricket week in August, the Canterbury Festival in September/October, and the twice-yearly (Easter and summer) Chaucer Festival. Details from the Tourist Information Centre, which can also arrange guided tours of the city.

As well as being an attractive centre in its own right, Canterbury is an ideal base from which to explore the Kent countryside and coastline. Small resorts like Whitstable and Herne Bay between them offer facilities for sailing, water-skiing and indoor sports, as well as plenty of amusements for children. Also in the area is the largest breeding colony of gorillas in the world (at Howlett's Zoo, Bekesbourne); Blean Bird Park; Chilham Castle, where medieval jousting tournaments are held; and Leeds Castle near Maidstone, built on two small islands in a lake and with a variety of attractions in its extensive grounds.

The architecture of the city is a constant reminder of its past: the Weaver's Houses (above, left) were the home of Flemish and Huguenot refugees; Canterbury Museum (above, right) is housed in the former Poor Priests' Hospital; Christ Churchgate and Memorial (below, right); and Westgate Gardens (below, left).

THE ROYAL PAVILION
Brighton, East Sussex

Onion-shaped domes, spires and minarets in the Indian Moghul style are not what immediately spring to mind when the seaside resort of Brighton is first mentioned, but they characterise one of the town's most famous landmarks.

King George IV's Royal Pavilion was originally a simple Classical-style villa designed by Henry Holland and built – when the future monarch was still the Prince of Wales – in 1787. Nearly 30 years later it was rebuilt in its present form to the ornate and exotic plans of John Nash. George IV used the Pavilion as his seaside palace until 1827 and his brother, William IV, also spent much time

there. Queen Victoria decided it was not private enough for her taste, and took many of the furnishings with her when she left it for the last time in 1845.

The Indian exterior of the Pavilion is fantastic enough but the interior – decorated in the Chinese style popular when the original villa was built – is just as spectacular. Many of the items that left with Queen Victoria have now been returned from Buckingham Palace and Windsor Castle, and furniture and paintings on permanent loan from Queen Elizabeth II help to ensure that the Pavilion now appears much as it did when it was a royal residence. It is open to the public every day (except Christmas and Boxing Day), though times vary according to the season.

The Royal Pavilion (opposite page) is perhaps Brighton's most unusual landmark.

The Banqueting Room at the Royal Pavilion.

Conical-roofed oasthouses topped by white-painted cowls are typical of the Kentish landscape.

WHITBREAD HOP FARM
Beltring, near Paddock Wood, Kent

There has been a working hop farm at Beltring ever since the mid-16th century, when the crop was first introduced to help satisfy England's growing thirst for beer. Today Whitbread Hop Farm has what is said to be the finest collection of Victorian oast-houses in the world and, as well as still being a working farm, its museums and craft workshops set out to recapture some of the rural ways of life which have long since vanished elsewhere.

The Hop Museum is set in a traditional oast house. Photographic exhibitions, a video show, displays of period costume and the tools of the trade all come together to trace the development of hop farming over the past 100 years. Items collected and used by one local family are displayed in the Rural Craft Museum, while the Agricultural Museum features bygones with farming connections.

'Live' attractions include regular visits from craftsmen demonstrating their skills, and special events – including a country-and-western festival, Beltring Fayre and the

Hop Festival – are held throughout the season, which runs from early April until early November.

Whitbread Hop Farm is also home to some of the brewery's famous Shire horses, which still haul drays carrying beer-barrels as well as the ceremonial coach in the Lord Mayor of London's annual pageant. Young horses are brought up here until, at the age of four years (and weighing nearly a ton), they start training for their working lives; retired and 'holidaying' animals are also based here.

MONK'S HOUSE
Rodmell, near Lewes, East Sussex

Three miles south of Lewes, near Rodmell village church, is Monk's House, once the home of Virginia and Leonard Woolf. Virginia (1882–1941) wrote a number of innovative novels whose stream-of-consciousness technique and psychological penetration broke new ground.

Monk's House, a small converted farmhouse, still contains furniture and personal items that belonged to the Woolfs, and the garden has been restored. Now a National Trust property, but administered and maintained by its tenant, it is open on Wednesday and Saturday afternoons throughout the year. Times vary with the season.

TYRWHITT-DRAKE MUSEUM OF CARRIAGES
Maidstone, Kent

Housed in the 14th-century stables of what was once a residence for the archbishops of Canterbury is one of the finest collections of horse-drawn carriages in England.

From royal coaches to delivery carts, mail vans to street cabs, the collection spans almost 300 years from the late 17th century. State, official and private carriages, some on loan from HM Queen Elizabeth II, are on display along with livery and other associated memorabilia.

Admission to the collection is free. The museum is open all year, though opening times depend on the day of the week and the season.

The former stables of the Archbishop of Canterbury now house a unique collection of more than 50 horse-drawn vehicles in their original state.

THE ROYAL HORTICULTURAL SOCIETY'S GARDEN Wisley, Surrey

Wisley is the headquarters of the Royal Horticultural Society and an important research centre, a mecca for horticulturalists both amateur and professional. Half of Wisley Gardens' 300 acres is planted with a wide variety of trees, shrubs and plants which look particularly magnificent in spring (when rhododendrons and azaleas are in bloom) and autumn. Part of the remainder is used for growing new varieties of fruit and vegetables under experimental conditions, and student gardeners are trained here.

Cultivated and natural beauty abound. Rose and rock gardens, ponds, small model gardens and specialist ones – like a garden suitable for the disabled – are all laid out, and there is plenty of inspiration even for those whose own gardens may be tiny.

Many of the plants found at Wisley are rare in England, and the Plant Centre sells a range of hardy plants, fruit and bulbs, many of which are not available elsewhere. Glasshouse and conservatory plants are also on sale. Expert assistance on gardening matters is on hand at the Information Centre.

Wisley Gardens are open all year round, though closing times vary with the season. A cafeteria and licensed restaurant supply refreshments every day except for a couple of weeks around Christmas.

THE WEALDWAY

The Wealdway is an 80-mile footpath through the stunning beauty of the Kent and Sussex countryside, and runs between Gravesend and Eastbourne. The route takes in downland, woods, meadows, old lanes, tiny villages, rivers and vast sweeping views, all accessible via public rights-of-way.

Created by the Ramblers' Association – and maintained by them in association with the Wealdway Committee, the Countryside Commission and local authorities – the Wealdway has brought many little-known pathways back into use. It links up with seven other official long-distance routes, including the North and South Downs ways; like them, it can be travelled as a whole or short sections 'dipped into' here and there.

Available from the Wealdway Committee are guides to the route and to access points, car parking, public transport and overnight accommodation along the way.

Wander around Wisley Gardens (opposite page) and enjoy the dazzling display of colour and texture.

Japanese azaleas in full bloom on Battleston Hill.

1956 Hawker Hunter at Tangmere Military Aviation Museum.

The critical air battles of 1940 are the main theme of the Battle of Britain Hall, which contains the remains of aircraft, personal effects, photographs and paintings from both sides of the conflict. Tangmere's own history is illustrated with words, pictures and models in Tangmere Hall: children especially can have fun here with Spitfire and helicopter flight simulators. Middle Hall exhibits include models of the Mohne Dam and the 'Bouncing Bomb', uniform displays and memorabilia of a number of Royal Air Force regiments.

Tangmere is open to the public between early March and the end of October; there is ample free parking on site and a grassed picnic area around a restored Hawker Hunter fighter.

TANGMERE MILITARY AVIATION MUSEUM

Tangmere Airfield, near Chichester

Once a famous Battle of Britain airfield, Tangmere is now home to a museum telling the story of military flying from its earliest days to the present – with a special emphasis on the RAF's time at Tangmere and the airfield's role in the air war over southern Britain between 1939 and 1945.

Adams tank and observation car (below).

THE BLUEBELL RAILWAY

Sheffield Park Station, near Uckfield, East Sussex

Five miles of standard-gauge railway track, part of what used to be the British Rail route from East Grinstead to Lewes, still see steam

trains carrying passengers through the Sussex countryside.

Over the last 30 years, volunteer railway enthusiasts have ensured the preservation of the track itself and the trains that run along it. Repair workshops and carriage-shed facilities are fully operational, and now service the largest collection of locomotives and carriages in southern England.

The atmosphere of the steam-train era has been re-created at the stations at either end of the line. There is a small museum and shop at Sheffield Park, and a bookstall at Horstead Keynes; refreshment facilities include buffets at both stations, a self-service restaurant at Sheffield Park and a Victorian bar at Horstead Keynes.

Trains run every day from the beginning of June to the end of September, and on selected dates at other times of year. Even when no trains are scheduled, Sheffield Park Station is usually open for limited viewing. Special events are held throughout the summer, and the weekend Regency Belle offers Pullman-style wining and dining.

ARUNDEL TOY AND MILITARY MUSEUM *Arundel, West Sussex*

Old toys and games, teddy bears, puppets, dolls houses, mechanical and musical toys, model soldiers – these and all sorts of other reminders of children's playtimes from long ago are part of a vast private collection on display in a small Georgian cottage in Arundel's High Street.

The Arundel Toy and Military Museum is open most days between Easter and October, and on weekends only (or by special arrangement) in winter.

Enjoy a nostalgic trip back to childhood at the Arundel Toy and Military Museum.

BUCKLEYS MUSEUM OF SHOPS
Battle, East Sussex

Housed in a 600-year-old Wealden hall-house next to Battle Abbey, Buckleys Museum is a journey back to the time of gaslights and horse-drawn carriages, wind-up gramophones and china-faced dolls.

Over 30,000 exhibits dating from 1850 to 1950 are displayed in some of the settings they would have occupied in their time. Everyday objects, grown rare and quaint with age, are on the shelves of an arcade of Edwardian shops, and displayed within re-creations of a Victorian kitchen and a maid's room.

Buckley's Museum is open throughout the year, though times vary with the season.

Escape into a past era of gaslights and horse-drawn carriages at Buckleys Museum of Shops.

FOR FURTHER INFORMATION CONTACT:

Tourist Information Centre
34 St Margaret's Street
CANTERBURY
Kent
Telephone: (0227) 766567

London Tourist Board
26 Grosvenor Gardens
LONDON SW1W 0DU
Telephone: (071) 730 3488

South East England Tourist Board
1 Warwick Park
TUNBRIDGE WELLS
Kent TN2 5TA
Telephone: (0892) 40766

EAST ANGLIA

Colourful fishing boats at Aldeburgh, Suffolk.

The counties of Essex, Cambridgeshire, Suffolk and Norfolk cover a vast geographical area. There are few cities, towns are relatively far apart, and the over-riding impression the traveller gets here is that of open space over-hung with huge, constantly-changing skies.

Habitats ranging from open expanses of sandy heathland to thick forest characterise the Breckland landscape of Norfolk and Suffolk, and the Essex coastline has acres of saltings and mud flats that are a haven for many varieties of bird and plant life. Nature reserves throughout the area are maintained by a number of conservation bodies.

Glorious cathedrals at Ely, Peterborough and Norwich testify to a religious tradition going back a thousand years. It seems as if every village in East Anglia has at least one church – and sometimes a lonely church in a field is the only indication that a village once existed there. Two of the oldest, dating from Saxon times, are St Peter's Chapel (Bradwell, Essex) and one at Greensted, also in Essex. The great church-building period was the Middle Ages, when the cloth trade brought prosperity to the area – even some of the parish churches of this time were grand constructions. Suffolk examples include those at Lavenham, Long Melford and East Bergholt; wealth from agriculture and other forms of trade paid for the ones at Blythburgh, Southwold and Mildenhall.

An area so richly endowed with fertile agricultural land and a long coastline offers some superb local foodstuffs. Farm shops and roadside stalls sell local vegetables, and visitors are welcome to harvest seasonal produce from the many 'pick-your-own' farms in the region.

Beers from Adnams, Tolly Cobbold and Greene King are worth looking out for, as are those produced by small breweries based in the region. Vineyards at Pulham Market (near Diss, Norfolk), Chilford Hundred (Linton, Cambridgeshire), Saxmundham (Bruisyard Wines, Suffolk) offer tours, tastings and the chance to buy.

Local seafood specialities range from the exotic to the everyday. Colchester oysters and Cromer crabs are famous, as are cockles from Leigh-on-Sea. Fresh fish is available from ports all along the Suffolk coast, while smoke-houses throughout the region produce pale, delicately-flavoured kippers and other smoked fish.

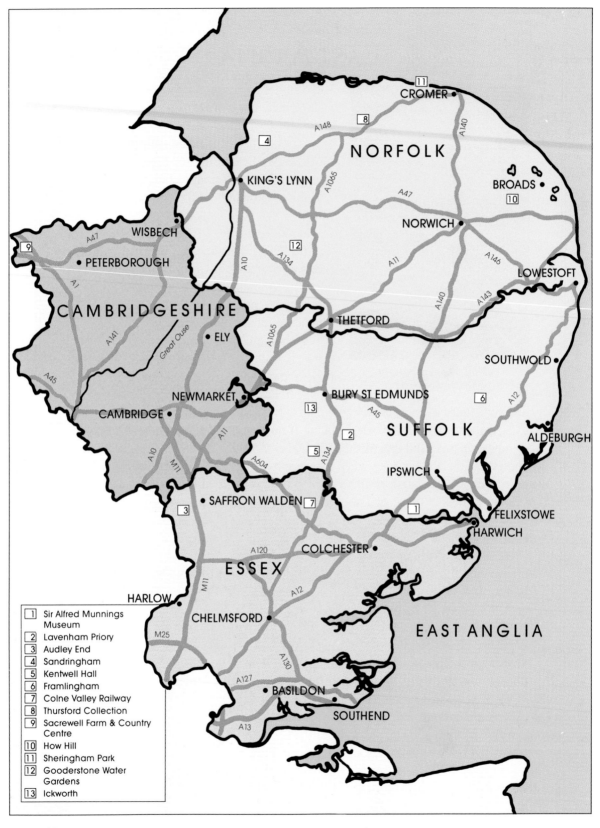

CROMER [11]

NORFOLK

[8]

A148

A140

[4]

KING'S LYNN

A1065

A10

A47

BROADS [10]

NORWICH

WISBECH

[9]

A47

[12]

A134

A11

A146

PETERBOROUGH

LOWESTOFT

A1

A140

A143

CAMBRIDGESHIRE

A1065

THETFORD

A141

ELY

SOUTHWOLD

Great Ouse

NEWMARKET

BURY ST EDMUNDS

[6]

A12

CAMBRIDGE

[13]

SUFFOLK

A45

A11

[2]

ALDEBURGH

A10

[5]

A134

M11

A604

IPSWICH

SAFFRON WALDEN

[7]

[1]

FELIXSTOWE

[3]

HARWICH

A120

COLCHESTER

ESSEX

M11

A12

HARLOW

M25

CHELMSFORD

EAST ANGLIA

A130

A127

BASILDON

A13

SOUTHEND

[1] Sir Alfred Munnings
    Museum
[2] Lavenham Priory
[3] Audley End
[4] Sandringham
[5] Kentwell Hall
[6] Framlingham
[7] Colne Valley Railway
[8] Thursford Collection
[9] Sacrewell Farm & Country
    Centre
[10] How Hill
[11] Sheringham Park
[12] Gooderstone Water
     Gardens
[13] Ickworth

How Hill Ludham,
near Great Yarmouth, Norfolk

Short residential courses designed to help visitors get to know the landscape, flora and fauna of the Norfolk Broads are held throughout the year at How Hill, which also hosts field courses for schools, colleges and environmental organisations.

How Hill is a thatched Edwardian house set in a 365-acre estate, most of which is an officially designated nature reserve. Reed beds, marshes, a small Broad, woodland, a reach of the River Ant, a marshman's cottage and three restored windmills all form part of How Hill, as do the house's own gardens.

Residential courses include the opportunity to explore the local countryside and coastland in the company of expert tutors, and find out about the wildlife – and ways of life – unique to the area. Each concentrates on a particular theme, takes participants out and about to places of interest, and most include evening talks and slideshows. Painting and drawing weekends offer amateur artists the opportunity to develop their skills.

Courses ranging from painting and drawing to the natural history of the Broads are held throughout the year at How Hill.

Lavenham's majestic church (top, right), and its lovely timber-framed buildings (below, right and opposite), remind present-day visitors of the town's past inhabitants, wealthy 15th- and 16th-century clothiers.

Course fees include tuition, excursions, meals, and centrally-heated accommodation. Unfortunately How Hill cannot guarantee fine weather: take waterproofs and wellingtons!

COLNE VALLEY RAILWAY
Castle Hedingham, Essex

Bought from British Rail in 1973 by a group of enthusiasts, the mile-long section of track along which the trains of the Colne Valley Railway now run was once part of the London and North Eastern Railway (LNER), later the Eastern Region of British Railways.

Nine years of weed growth had to be cleared, and track relaid, before locomotives could once more travel along the line. The station building was moved from its original site and rebuilt, brick by brick, in its present position; three bridges and a signal box have since been added. Now, in one of the prettiest parts of the Colne Valley, not far from the medieval village of Castle Hedingham, visitors are invited to experience rail travel as it used to be.

Vintage steam and diesel locomotives are on display, and there are regular fifteen-minute trips along the line aboard a steam-driven train. Restored carriages recapture the luxury of the Pullman days: one example came from the London-to-Paris *Golden Arrow*, another from the *Bournemouth Belle*. Both are now used as restaurant cars for lunches and dinners.

Events are held throughout the year, and include an Edwardian Extravaganza for which period costume is worn as well as summer and Christmas specials. Guided tours can be arranged by prior appointment.

LAVENHAM Suffolk

Lavenham is widely regarded as the finest surviving example of a medieval English town. A majestic church and some grand timber-framed buildings – lasting reminders of the wealthy clothiers who lived in the area during the 15th and 16th centuries – mingle, in typical medieval street patterns, with small cottages and crooked townhouses.

Over 300 buildings in Lavenham are listed as of architectural and historical interest, among them the Guildhall, the Old Wool Hall and many of the Church Street shops.

Lavenham Priory – formerly home to Benedictine monks, medieval wool merchants and an Elizabethan rector – is now owned by the Casey family, who have rescued it from the brink of collapse. A photographic exhibition traces the progress of their restoration work, and shows how the original timber-framed medieval hall-house became the 17th-century building which can be seen today.

Paintings, drawings and stained-glass windows by Ervin Bossayani (1891–1975) – responsible also for windows in England's Canterbury Cathedral and Washington Cathedral, US – can be seen throughout the Priory.

The Priory's Refectory Restaurant occupies what was once a blacksmith's store, and serves lunches and teas.

CAMBRIDGE Cambridgeshire

Though dominated by a university tradition going back to 1209, Cambridge was an important centre long before the first scholars arrived. Roman, Saxon and Norman settlers all left their mark, but it is the colleges – 32 in total, founded between 1284 and 1977 – where the city's architectural treasures are to be found. King's (founded 1441) and Trinity (1546) are among the finest. Visitors are welcome; guided tours can be arranged through the Tourist Information Centre.

Many fine museums contribute to Cambridge's academic reputation. The Fitzwilliam, one of the grandest, holds a variety of outstanding collections. Others worth a visit are the Folk Museum (local bygones), the Sedgewick Museum (geology), the University Museum of Archaeology and Anthropology, the Museum of Zoology and the Whipple Museum of Science. The Scott Polar Research Institute provides an insight into polar research and exploration, both past and present. Superb bookshops abound.

Interesting local churches include the Round Church, one of only four in England surviving from Norman times. The church of St Bene't, complete with Anglo-Saxon tower, is the oldest in Cambridgeshire.

Despite its links with the past, Cambridge is very much a living city. Kettles Yard Gallery mounts regular exhibitions of modern art throughout the year. Summer entertainment includes rowing races ('Bumps') and major international festivals celebrating the arts and folk music. Hire a punt, rowing boat or canoe from a local boatyard (open Easter to October) and explore the city's river, or travel up it to Grantchester, made famous by Rupert Brooke. Be warned, however – punting is a lot harder than it looks.

Though known for fine buildings, Cambridge has its share of open spaces too.

Punting is a favourite activity in Cambridge.

The Backs are a riot of spring colour, and offer superb views of the colleges across the river all year. Huge collections of plants are laid out in the tranquil gardens and houses of the Botanic Gardens (open all year); splendid views of both town and country can be enjoyed from Castle Mound, the grassy motte where William the Conqueror's castle once stood.

Within easy reach of Cambridge are a number of other interesting towns. Ely's magnificent cathedral soars over the flat Fens. The school in Huntingdon where Oliver Cromwell and Samuel Pepys were once taught now houses a museum. Newmarket, one of Britain's major horseracing centres, is home to the National Horseracing Museum. Agriculture, such a vital part of the area's life, is celebrated in one of the country's major annual festivals, the East of England Show at Peterborough (July).

Among the many historic buildings just out of town is Wimpole Hall, a spectacular 18th-century house set in a 350-acre park. An exhibition traces the Hall's development

from medieval manor to its present splendour; rare breeds of livestock are on show at Home Farm. Waymarked walks run through the park landscaped by Capability Brown.

The Mathematical Bridge at Queens' College (above); Cambridge market (below).

SIR ALFRED MUNNINGS ART MUSEUM

Castle House, Dedham, Essex

Suffolk-born painter Sir Alfred Munnings (1878–1959), specialist in the painting of horses and sporting scenes, lived and worked in Castle House for 40 years. A controversial and outspoken President of the Royal Academy from 1944–49, he was well known for his forthright criticisms of modern art.

Munnings' works hang in many public galleries, and Castle House contains the artist's studios as well as over 100 of his sketches, drawings and paintings. The house was opened to the public by his widow in 1961, as a tribute to her husband's memory. Visitors are welcome at specified times during the summer months.

Munnings is not the only East Anglian artist with a Dedham connection. Landscape painter John Constable (1776–1837) – like Munnings, the Suffolk-born son of a miller – went to school there. The village church of St Mary, built about 1500, appears in many of Constable's works.

ALDEBURGH Suffolk

A prosperous port until the 16th century, when east-coast seas and storms eroded its coastline and helped silt up its river's estuary, Aldeburgh is now famous as the site of the annual music festival started by composer Benjamin Britten in 1948.

Though the Festival, held at nearby Snape Maltings and various venues in the town, is perhaps the primary attraction for June visitors, the town itself is quaint and picturesque. The 16th-century timber-framed Moot Hall, now the Council Chamber, once dominated the centre of the town – that it is now almost on the sea-wall testifies to the extent of coastal erosion over 400 years.

On a warm summer's day, the typical 19th-century seafront houses and small high-street shops make strolling round the town a pleasure, but it is a very different, more dramatic, picture when storms lash the coast and the might of the North Sea is unleashed.

Not far up-river from Aldeburgh is the magnificent concert hall built on the site of the old Maltings at Snape. Musical and other events are held here throughout the year.

Those whose pleasures are gastronomic rather than cerebral should travel just down the coast to Orford. The renowned Butley–Orford Oysterage, one of England's finest fish smokers, is here – and though its oyster farm and smokery are not open to visitors, produce can be both sampled at the restaurant and bought at the shop.

Aldeburgh (right, and opposite page), home to the annual music festival, was a prosperous port until the 16th century.

SHERINGHAM PARK
Upper Sheringham, Norfolk

The 770-acre estate surrounding Sheringham Hall includes the 90-acre park designed by Humphry Repton (1752–1818), one of the most important Georgian landscape gardeners. English parks and gardens up to his time had been very formal; Repton and other influential designers helped develop a more naturalistic, picturesque approach which aimed at enhancing the existing landscape rather than imposing a strict man-made pattern upon it.

Sheringham Hall stands in the 90-acre park designed by Humphry Repton.

Sheringham Park is open all year round, from dawn to dusk every day. In May and June a large area of rhododendrons and azaleas create an especially fine display of colour. Numerous waymarked walks lead visitors through mature woodland, parkland and to the coast, and viewing towers offer spectacular vistas of both coast and countryside.

Repton – who lived for a time in nearby Aylsham – is thought by some to have been the architect of Sheringham Hall itself, though others think his son is more likely to have been responsible. Because the Hall is privately occupied (though the Park comes under the aegis of the National Trust), it is not open to the public. Selected rooms may be viewed only by special (written) arrangement with the leaseholder.

FRAMLINGHAM CASTLE
Framlingham, Suffolk

Roger Bigod, a poor Norman knight, built a fortified house in Framlingham on land given to him by King Henry I at the beginning of the 12th century. In 1136 his descendents were granted the Earldom of Norfolk and Hugh, the 1st Earl, began the transformation which eventually turned the house into a magnificent castle. His son, Roger, completed the work.

From the outside, Framlingham Castle now looks almost the same as it did when it was built. It was the most modern type of defence then known, with a continuous curtain wall linking thirteen towers instead of the more traditional Norman keep-and-bailey design. Later (Tudor) occupants added the chimneys which now crown most of the towers and parts of the wall.

In its time Framlingham Castle was the home of some of East Anglia's greatest families. Mary Tudor was proclaimed Queen of England there in 1553, and the last years of Elizabeth I's reign saw it functioning as a prison. As one monarch succeeded another it frequently changed hands.

The castle was eventually bequeathed to Pembroke College, Cambridge, on condition that a poorhouse be erected within its walls. Everything except the walls, gatehouse and towers was gradually demolished, and the 17th-century poorhouse – which survives intact – replaced the castle's Great Hall. Today the north wing of the poorhouse is home to a collection of local bygones.

Framlingham Castle (above). The poorhouse (left) was erected in the 17th century when the castle was bequeathed to Pembroke College, Cambridge.

THE THURSFORD COLLECTION
*Thursford Green, Thursford,
near Fakenham, Norfolk*

Said to be the finest collection of steam-driven engines in the world, the Thursford Collection includes road locomotives as well as the showmen's traction engines which used to power attractions at fairs around Britain. Ploughing and barn engines are also on show.

Gleaming in gilt, colourfully carved and wonderfully ornate, nine mechanical organs – and a classic Wurlitzer cinema organ – provide daily musical entertainments.

This unique gondola switchback, the only one of its kind surviving from the last century, is just one of Thursford's attractions.

Special events throughout the summer months feature a variety of guest organists as well as other musical entertainers.

Visitors can travel back to childhood aboard a switchback fairground roundabout, its Venetian-style gondolas restored to their original gilt and glittering colours, or take a ride on Thursford's narrow-gauge steam railway.

Old farm buildings have been transformed into shops selling local produce, mementoes of Thursford, and gifts; there is also a picture gallery. Teas, snacks and home-made ice-cream are on sale.

Sandringham House is the Royal Family's traditional Christmas holiday residence.

SANDRINGHAM Norfolk

The village of Sandringham is famous for Sandringham House, one of the English royal family's residences. The 19th-century house – bought by Edward, Prince of Wales, in 1861 – stands in its own extensive parkland and is the family's traditional Christmas holiday destination.

Sandringham House is only part of the royal estate, which includes the park and the royal parish church of St Mary Magdalene. Both house and gardens are open to the public at specified times from May to September, though the house is closed whenever any member of the royal family is in residence there.

Visitors are welcome to explore the estate's country park, nature trail and picnic areas, as well as to buy some of the plants grown in the royal gardens.

The church of St Mary Magdalene was extensively restored in 1857 and houses treasures given both by members of the royal family and their admirers. The organ was a gift from Edward VII, while two kings who later died at Sandringham House –

George V (in 1936) and George VI (1952) – presented the church with the oak roof of the nave and an unusual folding lectern. The church is open to visitors.

ICKWORTH Horringer, near Bury St Edmunds, Suffolk

Conceived by an eccentric bishop with a taste for art, travel and architectural flights of fancy, Ickworth features a 100-foot high oval rotunda and flanking wings. The bishop, Frederick Hervey, 4th Earl of Bristol and Bishop of Derry, proposed to live in the rotunda and display his fine collections of paintings and sculpture in the wings.

His plans were thwarted, however – first by Napoleon, who occupied Rome in 1797, imprisoned the unfortunate bishop who happened to be there at the time, and confiscated his collections; then by his own death, which intervened when the building was only half finished.

The project eventually took 36 years from design (1794) to its completion by the 5th Earl of Bristol in 1830. The house – and 2000 acres of the estate – was eventually

Ickworth was the conception of an eccentric bishop who had a taste for art, travel, and architectural flights of fancy.

handed to the National Trust in 1956.

As well as the remarkable rotunda, present-day visitors can enjoy Ickworth's fine collection of silver, Regency furniture and paintings. There are formal gardens and miles of waymarked walks through parkland landscaped in the 18th century by Capability Brown.

KENTWELL HALL
Long Melford, Suffolk

Kentwell Hall, built around 1563 by the Clopton family, is a mellow redbrick Tudor mansion surrounded by a broad moat. Nearly lost as a result of long neglect, it became a privately-owned family home in 1971 and is open to the public at selected times between Easter and October.

Almost twenty years' work restoring both Hall and gardens to their former splendour are now bearing fruit. Many rooms have been refurbished and furnished, and work continues. The exterior of the house remains as it was in the 16th century, though its interior reflects the changing tastes of a succession of owners.

A collection of Tudor-style costumes recalls the hall's heyday, while regular events through the summer months intro-

duce visitors to the area's history by re-creating everyday Tudor life. Up to 200 costumed participants, representing folk from all walks of life, carry on what would have been typical occupations of the time. Visitors are welcome to engage them in conversation about their lives and work, and discuss the pressing issues of their day.

Permanent attractions include the 17th-century walled gardens, a brick-paved maze, and a working model farm based on rare livestock breeds, relocated Tudor buildings and old tools and equipment.

Kentwell Hall has undergone extensive restoration over the past twenty years, and is now the venue for regular summer events.

NORWICH Norfolk

A prosperous and important city for over a thousand years, Norwich is still a busy commercial and shopping centre with a flourishing cultural life. The buildings of the old city cluster around the cathedral, set in the largest cathedral close in Britain. Though most of it dates from Norman times, the cathedral's elegant 315-foot spire – the second highest in England after Salisbury – was added 400 years later. Also in the Close is the 14th-century Norwich School, where Horatio Nelson was a pupil.

Nearby Tombland was once Norwich's Saxon market-place. The city still hosts the largest open-air market in England, though it is now on a site overlooked by Norwich Castle, one of the finest examples in England of Norman military architecture. Its museum houses works by the Norwich School of artists (including Crome and Cotman), archaeological and natural history exhibits – and the best specialist collection of British ceramic teapots in the world.

Two faces of Norwich – the Cathedral (right) and busy London Street (below).

The river at Norwich is part of the 200 miles of waterways that make up the Norfolk Broads.

Anglia, where the award-winning Sainsbury Centre for Visual Arts houses a number of important collections and is a 20th-century architectural landmark.

Because the city centre of Norwich is so compact, it is easy to explore on foot. Good pubs and other refreshment stops abound. The central traffic-free shopping area extends down medieval passageways like Bridewell Alley, where Colman's famous Mustard Shop and Museum can be found. Guided tours and suggestions for self-directed walks are available from the Tourist Information Centre, sited in the 14th-century Guildhall in the market place.

As well as being worth a visit in its own right, Norwich is an excellent base from which to explore Norfolk. There are many quiet sandy beaches along the coast, though Great Yarmouth, sixteen miles away, is a traditional bustling seaside resort. Six miles north of the city, Wroxham is a central spot from which to take a boat and travel some of the 200 miles of lakes and waterways that make up the Norfolk Broads. Further afield are the stately homes and gardens of Blickling Hall, Felbrigg, Houghton and Holkham, and museums throughout the county cover interests ranging from rural life to steam engines.

Other city museums cover domestic life (Strangers Hall) and local industry (Bridewell). The church of St Peter Hungate, close to the restored medieval street of Elm Hill, houses displays of ecclesiastical art and furnishings, and is only one of 33 pre-Reformation churches that still remain within the city's ancient walls. Regular musical events and antique fairs are held in the halls of what were once the huge monastery churches of St Andrew's and Blackfriars.

A wide variety of entertainment features on the Theatre Royal's year-round programme, while classics are the main bill of fare at the Elizabethan-style Maddermarket Theatre. The Norwich Puppet Theatre has its home in a converted medieval church, and the Norwich Arts Centre hosts regular contemporary arts events of all kinds. On the outskirts of the city is the University of East

SACREWELL FARM AND COUNTRY CENTRE *Thornhaugh, Peterborough*

Sacrewell's first arrivals were ancient Britons who camped by its stream around 8000 years ago. Evidence of their presence — and of the Romans who followed — continues to surface in the shape of flint tools and weapons, as well as pottery and coins, when local land is ploughed.

Present-day visitors to Sacrewell find a 500-acre working farm administered by a charitable trust devoted to agricultural improvement, education and research.

As well as tours of the farm which illustrate the intensity and efficiency of

NORWICH

Norwich has a wealth of attractions for its visitors: the market (left), open daily; Colman's Mustard Shop (above and right); and Elm Hill (below), the restored medieval street.

20th-century agriculture, there are ample reminders of earlier days. Sacrewell's working watermill is said to date back to the Domesday Book (1086), while domestic and agricultural bygones from more recent times are displayed in 18th-century farm buildings.

Other collections also feature the way people used to live and work in the area. Themes include traditional country crafts and skills, tools, motive power, shelter, and domestic life.

AUDLEY END
Saffron Walden, Essex

Open to the public between the beginning of April and the end of September, Audley End is an elegant Jacobean mansion standing in its own grounds – grounds which were originally landscaped by Capability Brown in the 18th century, and which now contain a mile-long miniature railway.

Audley End, the beautiful Jacobean Mansion, was once twice its present size.

At the time it was built – in 1603 by Lord Howard of Walden, First Earl of Suffolk – Audley End was about twice its present size and one of the largest houses in England. Sir John Vanbrugh was the architect who supervised its drastic remodelling early in the 18th century, though he kept the graceful exterior and original Great Hall.

The interior of the house fell into some disrepair towards the end of the 18th century, but was restored and redecorated by occupants Sir John Griffin Griffin (advised by architect Robert Adam) and the 19th-century owner, the 3rd Lord Braybrooke.

Capability Brown turned the gardens into one of the finest landscaped parks in the country, to which Adam contributed a circular temple and bridge. The Jacobean stables now house a display featuring Victorian agriculture, a collection of old wagons and the estate's own fire engine.

GOODERSTONE WATER GARDENS
Gooderstone, near Swaffham, Norfolk

Seven acres of privately-owned gardens, complete with flowers, shrubs, grassy walks, pools, bridges and a lake, are open to the public between Easter and the end of October at Gooderstone.

Owner Bill Knights, now in his 80s, developed the site from what was once nothing more than a boggy meadow behind his carrot factory. It is not the easiest of places to find – off the A47 between Swaffham and Stoke Ferry, not far from Oxborough Hall – but its glorious spectacle of colour is worth looking for.

From June until the end of September, all proceeds raised from Sunday visitors go to charity.

FOR FURTHER INFORMATION CONTACT:

Tourist Information Centre
Guildhall
Gaol Hill
NORWICH NR2 1NF
Telephone: (0603) 666071

Tourist Information Centre
Wheeler Street
CAMBRIDGE CB2 3QB
Telephone: (0223) 322640

East Anglia Tourist Board
Toppesfield Hall
HADLEIGH
Suffolk IP7 7DN
Telephone: (0473) 822922

EAST MIDLANDS

Bakewell, Derbyshire

It seems that everywhere in Britain there are contrasting counties and none more so than the counties of Derbyshire, Nottinghamshire, Northamptonshire and Lincolnshire.

Derbyshire is a land of lowlands to the south east, while to the north west are the high peaks and low vales of the Peak District. This rough moorland is renowned for its beauty and was the first in Britain to be made a National Park in 1951. The area has some of the highest land in the country – Kinder Scout stands at 2088 feet and Buxton, at just over 1000 feet above sea-level, is one of the highest towns in England. This wild beauty was inspiration to Jane Austen whose novel *Pride and Prejudice* is thought to be based around Bakewell.

In contrast Nottinghamshire – one of the few surviving mining areas – is mostly lowlands, while the land to the west rises to the uplands of the Pennines. In the south west is Sherwood Forest which although greatly diminished still contains some beautiful oak woodlands. For centuries the county has been the home of so many Dukes it has been called the 'Dukeries'. Today there are several of these vast estates open to the public including the Duke of Newcastle's estate at Clumber.

Lincolnshire is mainly marsh and fenland but with some hills towards the Humber. The flat land is dotted with windmills, bulb fields and Lincoln red cattle which graze under vast skyscapes. Standing over this flat plain is the ancient city of Lincoln, dominated by its 11th-century cathedral. This is the third largest cathedral in England and appears to tower above the city, an effect that is heightened by its position, on the summit of the hill leading into the city.

Leicestershire and Northamptonshire are both agricultural counties. Northamptonshire has several historic houses, including Althorp, the former home of the Princess of Wales. Museums around the counties include the Northampton and Kettering Museum where the history of footwear – a trade for which the county is noted – is exhibited; while at Corby there is a Steel-Making Heritage Centre demonstrating this aspect of the county's industrial heritage.

Favourite county dishes include Bakewell Tart which, it is claimed, was first made at the Rutland Arms Hotel in Bakewell. Local produce includes the Bramley apple – first grown in Southwell near Nottingham. A much sought after product of the area is bottled Buxton Spring Water which comes from 5,000 feet below the Derbyshire Peaks.

EAST MIDLANDS

DERBYSHIRE

LINCOLNSHIRE

NOTTINGHAMSHIRE

• GAINSBOROUGH

• BUXTON
3
• CHESTERFIELD

• BAKEWELL
4

• LINCOLN

• MANSFIELD
7

NEWARK-ON-TRENT

8

10

11
• NOTTINGHAM

9

• BOSTON
2

DERBY •
LONG EATON •

• GRANTHAM

• LOUGHBOROUGH

LEICESTERSHIRE

Rutland Water

• LEICESTER

5

• HINCKLEY

• KETTERING

NORTHAMPTONSHIRE

• WELLINGBOROUGH
NORTHAMPTON

6

STOKE BRUERNE
1

1	Stoke Bruerne Canal Museum
2	Boston Guildhall
3	Chatsworth
4	Haddon Hall
5	Rockingham Castle
6	Sulgrave Manor
7	Sherwood Forest
8	Heights of Abraham
9	Battle of Britain Memorial Flight
10	White Post Modern Farm
11	Lace Hall

HADDON HALL Derbyshire

Restored at the beginning of the 20th century following around 200 years of neglect, Haddon Hall was the main country residence of the early Dukes of Rutland. Sympathetically refurbished to re-create its medieval splendour, it is now the family's Derbyshire seat and open to the public between the end of March and the beginning of October. Special events, chosen for their relevance to Haddon's historical setting, take place in the Hall's grounds throughout the open season.

The oldest parts of the present house date from the 13th century, though there was a dwelling on the same site even before then.

Among its treasures are a 14th-century chapel where fine frescos adorn the walls, and the kitchens and Great Hall where time appears to have stood still for over 600 years. The Long Gallery, its 110-foot length panelled in oak and walnut, is testimony to the skill of 16th-century craftsmen.

Outside, Haddon's gardens are built on six great stone terraces stepped into the steep hillside leading down to the River Wye. Though the gardens were replanted when the Hall was restored, their 17th-century structure has been carefully maintained. Clematis and scented roses bloom in profusion in the height of summer, though the garden provides plenty of interest throughout the growing season.

Haddon Hall is one of the best preserved medieval houses in Britain.

A carving over a door to workshops in the Lace Market area of Nottingham.

The Canal Museum (opposite page) features displays based on the history of the River Trent.

The Lace Centre, Nottingham, where visitors can learn about the history of lace-making and buy lace products.

THE LACE HALL Nottingham

Nottingham's fame as a centre for lace-making is worldwide. Standing in the city's Lace Market, once the hub of the 19th-century lace-making industry, is the former Unitarian Chapel that now houses the Lace Hall and its permanent 'Story of Nottingham Lace' exhibition.

Lace-making, both by hand and machine, is demonstrated in authentic period settings with the help of an award-winning audio-visual show. From the Lace Shop, visitors can buy Nottingham Lace products ranging from cushions through lingerie

to bridal dresses; also on sale are a range of books, prints, lace-making equipment and souvenirs.

The Lace Hall is open all year round (except Christmas Day and Boxing Day), and refreshment facilities are available.

THE CANAL MUSEUM Stoke Bruerne, near Towcester, Northamptonshire

Two centuries of canal history are brought to life at Stoke Bruerne's Canal Museum. Housed in a restored canal-side cornmill, the museum features working models, exhibits and archive film that vividly re-create the way the boatmen and their families lived.

Holiday craft ply what is still one of the liveliest stretches of the Grand Union Canal, and contrast vividly with the traditional working narrowboats of a bygone age. Boat trips, towpath walks and free guided tours introduce visitors to the history of the area, and staff are always on hand to answer questions. Blisworth Tunnel, the longest tunnel still navigable today, is not far away.

Picturesque Stoke Bruerne itself, one of the best known examples of a canal village, plays host throughout the year to a wide variety of events and exhibitions. These range from canal craft fairs and exhibitions of waterway art to Easter Egg hunts and Morris dancing.

SULGRAVE MANOR
Near Banbury, Oxfordshire

Sulgrave manor is a fine example of a modest manor house and garden of the time of Shakespeare, and was once home to the ancestors of George Washington, first President of the United States of America.

It was a Washington who bought the Manor from Henry VIII in the 16th century, and who built the present house. Though furnished – in contrast to the more austere look of the third, the Tudor Great Chamber.

Outside, Sulgrave's gardens range from the decorative to the functional. Roses and lavender perfume the air, and the kitchen garden recalls a time when it supplied fresh vegetables for the table. A herb garden takes the form of an Elizabethan knot; formal topiary surrounds well-kept lawns, and a paddock provides a picnic area for today's visitors.

Sulgrave Manor (below) was built by a 16th-century ancestor of George Washington. Although the latter never lived here, there are portraits of him in the Great Hall (opposite page) and in the Oak Parlour.

now a museum, it retains a lived-in, family home atmosphere. Each room has been furnished in either Tudor or Queen Anne style, and there are many reminders of Sulgrave's famous connections.

A fully-furnished 18th-century kitchen is complete with open hearth and cooking equipment of the time. Upstairs, the two 18th-century bedrooms are elegantly

Sulgrave Manor's Visitor Centre now occupies what used to be the property's Brew House, where refreshments are available in 18th-century surroundings. Upstairs in the loft is a museum tracing the development of the Manor and the village. Both Manor and Visitor Centre are open six days a week from the beginning of February to the end of December, though times vary with the season.

LINCOLN Lincolnshire

When the Romans invaded Britain they appropriated the Celtic hill fort at Lincoln, changed its name, and established what was then one of the finest cities in the country. Though their street level is now eight feet below ground, traces of their presence remain above it in the form of parts of city walls, and monumental gateways like Newport Arch and the Lower West Gate; excavations are gradually revealing other relics.

Lincoln's historic centre remains remarkably untouched. Narrow medieval streets, like the Strait, Steep Hill and Bailgate, contain many interesting and historic buildings. What is thought to be England's oldest inhabited building – Jew's House on Steep Hill – dates from the 12th century, when the Normans were encouraging Jews to settle in prosperous towns and help finance local trade.

The Norman influence is obvious, too, at Lincoln Castle, a great walled fortress with two massive towers, and in the west front of Lincoln Cathedral. Though most of the rest of this magnificent building dates from the prosperous 13th century, by which time Lincoln was an important centre for the cloth trade, it was originally the seat of a Norman diocese stretching all the way from the Humber to the Thames. Superb carvings, many fine architectural features and ancient stained glass are among Lincoln Cathedral's many treasures.

Greyfriars City and County Museum is housed in what was once part of a 13th-

Lincoln Cathedral.

century complex of monastic buildings. Local history from prehistoric times to about 1750 is one speciality, natural history another. Highlights include a fine collection of prehistoric pottery, one of the four original copies of Magna Carta still in existence, and one of the most complete fossils ever found in Lincolnshire – a plesiosaur discovered in a local brickpit.

Other collections with local connections are held at the Museum of Lincolnshire Life and the Usher Gallery, where watercolours by Peter de Wint capture the artist's fascination with the Lincolnshire countryside. Queen Victoria's Poet Laureate was one of Lincoln's famous sons, and the Tennyson Research Centre within the City Library houses one of the most important Tennyson collections in the world, complete with family papers, original manuscripts, books, letters and illustrations. The National Cycle Museum contains some exhibits Tennyson might have recognised: as well as unicycles, dicycles, tricycles, sociables and quadricycles, there is a replica of a 19th-century cycle workshop and visitors can test their skill with a penny farthing.

Not far from Lincoln are some fine stately homes, such as the 17th-century Belton House, Doddington Hall, one of England's most beautiful Elizabethan mansions, and glorious Belvoir Castle. The flat Fens and the rolling Lincolnshire Wolds are within easy reach, as is the county's east coast with its safe, sandy beaches and nature reserves.

Lincoln has been an Anglian town, a
Danish borough, and a Norman
stronghold. Traces of its history are
seen in the walls (above); cobbled
streets (below, right); and a memorial
to the poet Tennyson, born in Lincoln.

*B*AKEWELL *Derbyshire*

Built almost entirely of warm, brown stone, the small market town of Bakewell lies in beautiful countryside in the sheltered valley of the Derbyshire Wye. Crossing the river since the 13th century is one of the oldest packhorse bridges in England, and the wooded hills surrounding the town make for fine walking country. The beauties of Dovedale, Monk's Dale, Monsal Dale and Lathkill Dale are not far away.

Bakewell's most impressive building is the Parish Church of All Saints, parts of which date from the 12th century. There is evidence here of an earlier, Anglo-Saxon church, and an 8th-century sculptured cross still stands in the churchyard.

Most of the wells from which Bakewell takes its name – the early town grew up around twelve mineral-water springs – have now run dry, though they are remembered every July and decorated in the ancient ritual of well-dressing. It is still possible, however, to swim at the 17th-century Bath House, supplied throughout the year with naturally heated spring water at a temperature of 15°C.

Author Jane Austen stayed at Bakewell's Rutland Arms Hotel while working on *Pride and Prejudice*, and it is said that Bakewell was her model for Lambton, where her hero Mr Darcy lived.

It was in the kitchens at the Rutland Arms that the famous Bakewell Tart originated. The story goes that the hotel cook misunderstood her mistress's instructions on how to make a particular pudding, but that the result was so successful that the mistake has been deliberately made ever since. The pudding shop in Rutland Square has been producing tarts to the original formula since 1859.

The prototype Bakewell tart is said to have been made by mistake in the 19th century.

ROCKINGHAM CASTLE
Near Corby, Northamptonshire

Built by William the Conqueror, and used as a royal fortress until 1530, Rockingham Castle was given to one Edward Watson by King Henry VIII. It is still the home of his ancestors.

Present-day Rockingham Castle reflects almost every century of its 900-year history. Norman towers guard the entrance to the mainly Elizabethan house which was built within the original castle walls. The Tudor Great Hall, with its displays of arms and armour, recaptures the days of the Civil War when Rockingham was occupied by Roundhead forces. Charles Dickens produced and acted in plays in the Long Gallery, which now houses fine furniture and pictures. A collection of 20th-century art brings the castle right up to date.

Sweeping lawns and a rose garden occupy the site of what was once the castle's Old Keep. Twelve acres of gardens include the Wild Garden, a ravine containing over 200 species of trees and shrubs, and offer views across four counties. Home-made cream teas are available.

Rockingham Castle is open to the public on selected afternoons between Easter and the end of September.

THE WHITE POST MODERN FARM
CENTRE Near Newark, Nottinghamshire

Twelve miles north of Nottingham is a working farm which offers visitors the chance to get acquainted with a wide variety of modern agricultural systems, the farming countryside, and the animals raised in it.

Displays and exhibits emphasise the link between farming and the food we eat, show how a modern farm works, and what it can produce. Close contact with the farm animals is encouraged, and visitors can also safely explore modern farm machinery. Baby chicks, hatched with the help of an 8,000-egg incubator, can always be seen, and there is an outdoor pig-breeding unit. Free-range chickens, ducks and geese roam the lakeside picnic area, and refreshments are available in the tea gardens.

The White Post Modern Farm Centre is open all year round (not Mondays, apart from bank holidays), and guided tours can be arranged by appointment.

Charles Dickens was a frequent visitor to Rockingham Castle (above) and is said to have used it as a model for Chesney Wold in Bleak House.

THE HEIGHTS OF ABRAHAM
Matlock Bath, Derbyshire

Above the Derwent Valley, in the heart of Derbyshire's Peak District, the Heights of Abraham are reached via a spectacular cable car ride which starts at Matlock Bath railway station. Access to all the attractions within the 35-acre clifftop woodland is included in the price of the cable car ticket.

Panoramic views, play and picnic areas, woodland walks and water cascades are here, as well as the chance to learn more about what lies underground. An exhibition introduces the geology of the area, and tells the story of its development from prehistoric times. There are two great caverns to explore, and a re-creation of a working Derbyshire lead mine.

On the surface, the Tree Tops Visitor Centre offers refreshment facilities including a licensed bar-restaurant, a gift shop, and magnificent views from its terrace. The cable car and the Heights of Abraham are open daily from Easter to the end of October, and at certain times during the rest of the year.

BUXTON Derbyshire

The highest town in England, and one of the country's oldest spas, Buxton lies in the heart of Derbyshire's Peak District amid some glorious unspoilt scenery. Buxton's mineral waters bubble up to the surface at a constant 28°C and it was their presence that first attracted the Romans to the place, though it was not until the late 18th century that the 5th Duke of Devonshire developed the town to rival Bath as a fashionable spa.

Buxton's sweeping crescent is a fine sight, and the town's architectural centrepiece. Built close to the original St Anne's Well, it houses the Natural Baths which stand on the site of a Roman bath. Here about a quarter of a million gallons of warm, pale blue water

An officer of General Wolfe likened the wooded gorge of Derwent to the Quebec battlefield of 1759, thus giving it the name of Heights of Abraham.

Broadwalk in Buxton (opposite page), England's highest town.

gush every day into a marble basin from nine springs thought to be between 3,500 and 5,000 feet underground.

Also in the crescent is the world's only permanent exhibition devoted to the microscopic wonders of the natural world. Buxton Micrarium (open daily from the end of March to early November) features the tiny structures that come together to make animals, vegetable matter and minerals that can actually be seen. Over 400 microscopes, specially designed so that visitors can operate them, project what they 'see' onto television-sized screens. Tiny living forms are revealed as they act out their normal life cycles; crystals grow and develop into minerals, tracing out intricate designs as they do so.

Pleasure seekers have visited Buxton for years in search of a variety of entertainment. Buxton Pavilion's concert hall and ballroom are set in 23 acres of grounds where there are putting and bowling greens, tennis courts and a boating lake. The town's Edwardian 900-seat opera house has been restored in recent years. Buxton Museum houses extensive collections of local rocks and fossils, and includes ornaments made from one of the area's best known minerals, Blue John. In the hills surrounding the town, some of the caverns where minerals were mined are open to the public.

BATTLE OF BRITAIN MEMORIAL FLIGHT RAF Coningsby, Lincolnshire

At RAF Coningsby, the Battle of Britain Memorial Flight operates five Spitfires, two Hurricanes, and one of the only two Lancasters still flying today. The collection is maintained as a tribute to those fliers and ground crew who gave their lives in World War Two, and mounts shows and exhibitions all over Britain during the summer months.

When not flying, the Flight welcomes visitors to see its aircraft and collection of wartime memorabilia at RAF Coningsby where experienced guides are on hand to conduct tours and answer questions.

Open on weekdays (apart from two weeks over Christmas, and bank holidays), the site also features a large visitor centre, well-stocked souvenir shop and refreshment facilities. Because of operational commitments, the Flight cannot guarantee that all its aircraft will always be on show, and suggests that prospective visitors should telephone for details before arriving.

RUTLAND WATER Leicestershire

The largest man-made lake in western Europe covers 3,100 acres and has 27 miles of shoreline. As well as supplying water for domestic and commercial consumers in the region's large towns, it is an established water-sports and leisure centre. Two adventure playgrounds, conveniently located near major car parks, cater especially for children.

At the western end of Rutland Water is a 350-acre nature reserve, whose Lyndon Hill Visitor Centre is open on specified days between Easter and September. Displays, audiovisual programmes and bird watching hides have been created to introduce visitors to the wildlife of the area, where over 200 different species of birds have been recorded.

Rainbow and brown trout weighing over twelve pounds have been caught at Rutland Water, and the reservoir is said to be one of the finest fisheries in Europe. International competitions are held here; tuition for both beginners and experienced anglers – as well as permits and boat bookings – are all available locally.

Twenty-five miles of traffic-free waterside tracks offer cyclists the chance to explore all the main points of interest around Rutland Water. Bikes of all types to suit all ages can be hired. Regular passenger cruises aboard the *Rutland Belle* provide water-borne sightseeing opportunities, while those preferring to take to the water aboard their own craft –

whether dinghies or sailboards – have access to over 2,000 acres of it.

Rutland Water's history is the subject of a permanent exhibition at nearby Normanton Church Museum (open early April to the end of October).

CHATSWORTH *Derbyshire*

In a magnificent setting on the banks of the River Derwent in the Peak District National Park, Chatsworth is the home of the Duke and Duchess of Devonshire. Now one of the grandest country houses in England, it was originally built in 1555 for Bess of Hardwick, and was altered in the 17th century by her great-great-grandson, the 1st Duke of Devonshire. Later additions were made in the 19th century by the 6th Duke.

Chatsworth is richly furnished and decorated throughout with painted walls and ceilings, woodcarvings, elaborate inlay furniture and wall-hangings. Its collections of paintings, drawings, sculpture, silver, porcelain and curiosities are world famous.

Visitors are free to wander around the house at their own pace, following a clearly marked route which takes around an hour. A small charge is made for guided tours, which must be booked in advance.

Chatsworth's 100-acre garden is set in 1000 acres of parkland landscaped by Capability Brown. Visitors can enjoy its herbaceous borders, a rose garden, and secluded walks among rare shrubs and forest trees; a tropical greenhouse and some spectacular water features are among its more unusual surprises. Guided tours of the greenhouses, for which a charge is made, can be booked in advance.

Both house and garden are open daily (late morning onwards) between late March and late October. A licensed restaurant serves light refreshments, lunches and high teas when the house and garden are open. Of special interest to children are the farmyard and adventure playground, open daily

Storm clouds gather over Chatsworth House (opposite page).

between late March and the end of September, and weekends only during October. Gifts, home-grown plants and a variety of food products are on sale.

Spectacular special events take place from time to time during the summer months: details from Chatsworth.

THE GUILDHALL *Boston, Lincolnshire*

In medieval times, Boston was an important port for trade with Europe and the many fine buildings in the town are still a reminder of its early prosperity. Among them is the 15th-century Guildhall, once a meeting place and trading centre, later the Town Hall, and now a museum.

Because succeeding generations have adapted the building to suit their own purposes, the Guildhall reflects all periods from medieval to Georgian times. Some original stone mullioned windows have survived later alterations to its façade: those lighting the high-roofed Banqueting Hall on the first floor contain remnants of ancient stained glass depicting the twelve Apostles, and are a reminder that the room was originally designed as a chapel.

Prisoners awaiting trial in the Guildhall's Court Room were kept in two cells linked to it by a spiral staircase. Their best known occupants were some of the Pilgrim Fathers, arrested during an attempt to leave England for the United States in search of religious freedom.

The Guildhall's kitchen dates back to 1552, and has been restored and equipped to reflect its function in the 17th century.

Exhibits, both temporary and permanent, within the Guildhall cover archaeology, costume and textiles, ceramics, militaria, numismatics, fine art and local history. There are reminders, too, of famous people associated with Boston, and of the town's trading history.

SHERWOOD FOREST COUNTRY PARK AND VISITOR CENTRE
Edwinstowe, near Mansfield, Nottinghamshire

Robin Hood, the legendary outlaw who stole from the rich to give to the poor, is indelibly associated with the ancient woodland of Sherwood Forest. His connection with the area is celebrated by a colourful exhibition at the Forest's Visitor Centre, which interprets the legend and mounts a number of special events to help bring it to life.

The Visitor Centre is at the heart of the 450-acre oak woodland, the largest area of ancient oak forest in western Europe, where Hood and his merry men once roamed. Waymarked walks and footpaths lead through the forest, and help visitors find their way to The Major Oak, supposed to be the meeting place and hideout of Robin Hood and his Merry Men. Major Oak is situated a mile from Edwinstowe, where Robin Hood is said to have married Maid Marion.

Both Country Park and Visitor Centre are open all year round, though times vary according to the season.

FOR FURTHER INFORMATION CONTACT:

Tourist Information Centre
9 Castle Hill
LINCOLN
Lincolnshire LN1 3AA
Telephone: (0522) 29828

Tourist Information Centre
21 St Giles Street
NORTHAMPTON
Northamptonshire NN1 1JA
Telephone: (0604) 22677/34881
Ext 404

Tourist Information Centre
14-16 Wheeler Gate
NOTTINGHAM
Nottinghamshire NG1 2NB
Telephone: (0602) 470661

East Midlands Tourist Board
Exchequergate
LINCOLN
Lincolnshire LN2 1PZ
Telephone: (0522) 531521

Sherwood Forest, the largest area of ancient oak forest in Western Europe.

HEART OF ENGLAND

Naunton, Gloucestershire.

The counties of Gloucestershire, Hereford and Worcester, Shropshire, Staffordshire, and Warwickshire form the heart of England. Gloucestershire is a richly agricultural county producing wheat, barley and dairy produce while from Warwickshire, Hereford and Worcester come dairy produce, hops, soft fruit and vegetables (in the Vale of Evesham) and the world famous Hereford cattle. Shropshire is now chiefly an agricultural county but was once the chief iron-producing county in England, and the world's first cast iron bridge was built here in 1779 at Ironbridge. Staffordshire is most noted for its potteries which help make it the 'black country' of the 18th century. Today the coal fired potteries are gone and the air across the undulating lowlands and high northern moorlands is fresh.

The Romans were amongst the first to prosper from the area and reminders of their presence have been unearthed at Chedworth, and at Wall where there are the remains of a bath and posting station.

As a region which enjoyed enormous prosperity in the industrial revolution the Midlands contain many relics of that past. At Ironbridge Gorge Museum the full story is relived and other evidence of an affluent Victorian society can be found at Droitwich Spa Brine Bath which once catered for the healthy Victorians at leisure, but which has been refurbished for the more discerning modern visitor.

The Midland counties were heavily involved in the Civil War and many buildings mark this historic uprising. At Boscobel House in Shropshire is the hiding place of King Charles II. The area was also often in conflict with the Welsh, and castles at Clun, Shrewsbury, and Ludlow bear witness to the need for border defences.

Although an industrial area there are many places of natural beauty. Cannock Chase in Staffordshire is a leisure centre and wildlife resort affording dramatic views across the Trent Valley; Gloucestershire has the ancient Forest of Dean which lies between the rivers Severn and Wye; Worcester is divided by the Malvern Hills into two lowland plains, both sides of which are agricultural, the Vale of Evesham being second only to Kent as Britain's largest fruit and market gardening centre, and in spring the air is full of the aroma of fruit blossom.

As a prosperous agricultural and industrial area, hunting is a feature of the region. Local delicacies include various game dishes of venison and rabbit. Fish is another local favourite, and salmon from the Severn and Wye are renowned.

Luscious fruit and vegetables grown locally are also available in abundance.

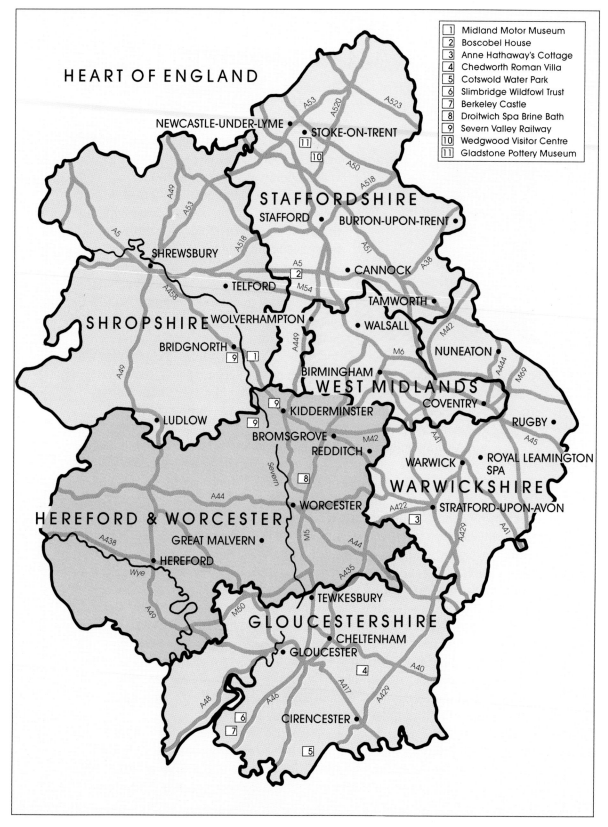

HEART OF ENGLAND

1	Midland Motor Museum
2	Boscobel House
3	Anne Hathaway's Cottage
4	Chedworth Roman Villa
5	Cotswold Water Park
6	Slimbridge Wildfowl Trust
7	Berkeley Castle
8	Droitwich Spa Brine Bath
9	Severn Valley Railway
10	Wedgwood Visitor Centre
11	Gladstone Pottery Museum

NEWCASTLE-UNDER-LYME
STOKE-ON-TRENT
STAFFORDSHIRE
STAFFORD
BURTON-UPON-TRENT
SHREWSBURY
CANNOCK
TELFORD
TAMWORTH
SHROPSHIRE
WOLVERHAMPTON
WALSALL
BRIDGNORTH
NUNEATON
BIRMINGHAM
WEST MIDLANDS
COVENTRY
LUDLOW
KIDDERMINSTER
RUGBY
BROMSGROVE
REDDITCH
ROYAL LEAMINGTON SPA
WARWICK
WARWICKSHIRE
HEREFORD & WORCESTER
WORCESTER
STRATFORD-UPON-AVON
GREAT MALVERN
HEREFORD
TEWKESBURY
GLOUCESTERSHIRE
CHELTENHAM
GLOUCESTER
CIRENCESTER

GLOUCESTER

A fortified harbour was built in Gloucester by the Romans in the first century AD for the invasion of Wales. Evidence of the city's occupation can be found at Eastgate Street, where Roman and medieval gate-towers and a moat can be seen in an underground exhibition chamber.

The Normans also occupied the city, and in 1089 built the cathedral with its huge 174 feet long nave. The cathedral was remodelled in the 14th century to accommodate the tomb of Edward II who was murdered in 1327 at Berkeley Castle, and today the transepts and choir are some of the earliest examples of perpendicular architecture.

The city has several museums such as the City Museum and Art Gallery on Brunswick Road, where exhibits include Roman coins, pottery, 18th-century walnut furniture and a late Iron Age bronze Birdlip mirror dating from AD25. The Folk Museum is situated on Westgate Street and here displays illustrate the social history, folklore, crafts and industries of the area. The Folk Museum is housed in a group of converted half-timbered houses and next door is the Old Custom House which is home to the Gloucestershire Regimental Museum where exhibits demonstrate the regiment's 290 years of service to the country.

Gloucester is linked by an enormous canal to docks at Sharpness sixteen miles away and is an important inland port. The story of transportation by river and canal is the feature of the National Waterways Musem at St Michael's Tower.

Other places of interest are Bishop Hooper's Lodging, where Bishop Hooper spent his final night before martyrdom in 1555; the Blackfriars Abbey which dates from the 13th century; the grave of Robert Raikes – founder of the Sunday School Movement – which can be seen at St Mary de Crypt Church; and the New Inn, a 15th-century pilgrim's hostel.

Gloucester Cathedral has some of the earliest and most beautiful perpendicular architecture in existence.

GLADSTONE POTTERY MUSEUM
Longton, Stoke-on-Trent, Staffordshire

During Victorian times Staffordshire was littered with potteries, but today Gladstone Pottery Museum is unique in that it is the only completely preserved 19th-century Victorian 'Potbank.'

The pottery contains the traditional machinery and equipment which are used both to demonstrate the skills of the potter and to enable potters to practise those skills. The cobbled yard outside contains four giant bottle ovens that were once used to fire the pottery but which are not in use today, as being coal-fired, they were one of the chief causes of the smog that earned the county the name of the 'black country.'

The pottery is now a museum, and contains galleries demonstrating the history of pottery. These include reconstructions of a Victorian potter's kitchen and bedroom and a range of pottery products produced over the years including decorative tiles. There is also a gallery depicting vintage toilets which has a working replica of the first water closet, designed for Elizabeth I by Sir John Harrington.

The pottery is situated three miles south east of Stoke-on-Trent and is open Monday to Saturday from 10-5pm and Sundays from 2pm-5pm with no admissions after 4.00pm and has a cafeteria.

Vintage lavatories (below) and ovens (left) are on view at Gladstone Pottery Museum.

MIDLAND MOTOR MUSEUM
near Bridgnorth, Shropshire

The Midland Motor Museum is located east of Bridgnorth in the old stable block set in the 24-acre grounds of Stanmore Hall. Exhibits include 100 vintage sports cars, racing cars and motorcycles dating from 1920 to 1980. The theme of the museum is the motor-racing circuit at Brooklands in Surrey, and many of the exhibits are cars that once raced there, but there are also Fords and Porsches which raced during the 1960s and 1970s at Le Mans.

Interesting exhibits include a 1925 Sunbeam Tiger 3978cc which in 1926 held the world land speed record of 152.33 mph, and a 24 litre Napier-Railton, in which John Cobb drove the fastest ever lap of 143.44 mph in 1933. The museum houses Jaguars, Ferraris, Bugattis and Porsches and many of these have been extensively rebuilt, but, it is claimed, most will still perform to the capacity to which they were designed.

Other exhibits are photographs, prints, spare parts, motoring memorabilia, and there is a motoring bookshop. The estate grounds are open for visitors to explore, and include picnic and play areas and a lakeside nature trail. There is also a camping park.

Both the museum and grounds are open daily.

WORCESTER

Worcester lies in the midst of rich farmland, but it is not agriculture that has gained the city its fame. Rather, it is the ancient manufacturing industries which over centuries have produced the famous Worcester sauce and the highly ornamental Worcester porcelain.

Porcelain was first manufactured by John Hall and his associates in 1751, and the Worcester porcelain industry soon became famous not only for its copies of Chinese and Japanese porcelains but for its original designs as well. Today the works in Severn Street and the Dyson Perrins Museum are open to the public by appointment. The factory tour demonstrates the process from raw material to finished product and the museum houses the world's best collection of Worcester porcelain dating from 1751.

The lovely 4th-century Worcester Cathedral overshadows the River Severn.

The Lea & Perrin Worcester sauce factory is in Midland Street and was founded by locals in 1825. The famous Worcester sauce – made to a recipe of the Governor of Bengal who was residing in Worcestershire – was first made five years after the business was formed.

The glove industry has been part of Worcester since the 13th century, and this industry still thrives today. The county also produces the Berrow's Worcester Journals, the world's oldest surviving newspaper, which was first published in 1690.

Worcester Cathedral overshadows the River Severn and the cricket ground. The crypt was built by the Normans but most of the remainder of the building was created in the 14th century. In 1216 the cathedral was the burial place of King John whose tomb carries the oldest royal effigy in England. Prince Arthur, the elder brother of Henry VIII, who died at fifteen, also lies here and the intricately carved Prince Arthur's Chantry was added by Henry VII in 1504 in memory of his son.

The city is full of history and places of interest including King Charles' house where the King hid before his flight after his defeat by Cromwell; the City Museum containing memorabilia from the Worcestershire Regiment and Yeoman Cavalry; Broadheath – now a museum – but once the home of composer Sir Edward Elgar whose work is regularly performed at the Three Choirs Festival; and the Guildhall, designed by Thomas White, a pupil of Sir Christopher Wren, which contains statues of Charles I, Charles II and Queen Anne.

Boscobel House
near Telford, Shropshire

Boscobel House was converted into a hunting lodge from a timber-framed farmhouse in the early 17th century by John Gifford, who was a Roman Catholic. Due to the religious controversy of the period the house incorporated several hiding places for priests.

During the Civil War the house harboured many Royalists and following his defeat at Worcester, Charles II hid on the estate before his flight to France. However it was too dangerous for the king to hide in the house which was searched by Cromwell's men by day, so instead he hid in an oak tree with his companion Major Carlos. A descendant of the tree – said to be grown from an acorn of the original – survives today and one of the priest's hiding places is said to have been the king's hideout for one night.

The house is situated ten miles east of Telford. It is furnished just as it was over 100 years ago in 1890 when the owners left and it was first opened to the public. The furniture is 17th-century, Georgian and Victorian.

Anne Hathaway's Cottage
Shottery, Warwickshire

A mile west of Stratford-upon-Avon in the village of Shottery is the childhood home and birthplace of Anne Hathaway, the wife of William Shakespeare and the mother of three of his children. The cottage was inhabited by the Hathaways until 1892 and is still linked to Stratford-upon-Avon by footpaths along which Shakespeare might have walked to visit Anne.

Today the timber-framed thatched cottage with latticed windows is a remarkable irregular building of stone, wattle and brick, part of which dates back to the 15th century. The cottage was damaged by fire in 1969, but has been carefully reconstructed and is open to the public.

Inside the cottage is furnished to the mid 16th-century period much as it would have been when Shakespeare courted Anne, before their marriage in 1582. In the living room is a wooden settle, on which it is claimed the couple sat in the cottage which was set in a typically English country garden.

The beautiful timber-framed thatched cottage that belonged to Anne Hathaway.

CHEDWORTH ROMAN VILLA
near Cirencester, Gloucestershire

Chedworth Roman Villa dates back to around AD 120 and is one of the best preserved villas in the country. Many of the original walls stand several feet high and have been heightened and re-roofed so the building is enclosed. The villa is set on a slope in over six acres of woodland in the Coln Valley close to the Roman road leading to Cirencester.

It is thought that the building once belonged to a rich landowner, as excavations have revealed a house with three wings around a courtyard. In Roman times the north wing was used to process Cotswold wool.

The house incorporates all the luxuries of a Roman residence including the hypocaust through which filtered the hot air underfloor heating – and two bathhouses. Present-day visitors can see some well-preserved mosaic floors. There is also a Nymphaeum, a water shrine lined with cement and filled by a natural spring which once supplied fresh water for the residents.

Well-preserved mosaic floors are amongst the treasures that can be seen at Chedworth Roman Villa.

With the fall of the Roman empire the villas in England were abandoned and forgotten; indeed Chedworth was only uncovered by accident in 1864 by a rabbiting party searching for a ferret. It was excavated in 1865 and today belongs to the National Trust. The villa contains a small museum where the many treasures found on the site such as stone carvings, coins and a pair of iron shears are displayed.

COTSWOLD WATER PARK
near Cirencester, Gloucestershire

The Cotswold Water Park is situated five miles south east of Cirencester and is an area of 1,500 acres comprising of almost 100 lakes created from disused gravel workings in the Upper Thames Valley. These lakes now support a variety of wildlife and are used for a range of activities including angling, bird watching, sailing, power boat racing and water sports.

The area includes the Neighbridge and Keynes Country Parks and a Nature Reserve, with numerous picnic sites, some with barbecues, which are linked by bridal ways

and footpaths. These are perfect for walking, bird watching or horse riding and in places some of the bridal path routes cut across the cycle paths to enable cyclists to experience rough terrain as well as even lanes. Keynes also has a children's beach and an adventure playground.

A special feature of the Somerford Lakes Reserve, is an hour-long guided tour around the 100-acre site in an Edwardian style launch. The tour includes an eel and trout farm and an island complete with resident wildlife.

Active visitors can hire equipment and participate in water sports as there are a number of sailing clubs with day ticket facilities and also angling clubs that sell day tickets for coarse and trout fishing.

Accommodation is available at Cotswold Hoburne where there is a camping and caravan site which has a club house, shop and swimming pool. The Country Park is open daily throughout the year, and the children's beach from the end of May until the end of September.

SLIMBRIDGE WILDFOWL TRUST
Slimbridge, Gloucestershire

Slimbridge is the headquarters of the Wildfowl Trust which was founded by naturalist Sir Peter Scott in 1946 to conserve wildlife and increase public awareness of the attraction of wildfowl.

The centre is situated four miles east of Sharpness and comprises of a 100-acre enclosure containing ducks, swans, and geese of almost every variety. Indeed, the Trust is home to a collection of over 160 different types of wildfowl, both resident and non-resident, which form the world's largest collection of wildfowl. One of the centre's most famous winter residents is the wild Bewick swan and the centre is also the winter home to around 7,000 white fronted geese and ducks from the arctic. The centre has paved level paths to enable easy access for wheelchairs and pushchairs.

The resident collection of birds come from across the world and include the Hawaiian goose or Nene, all six types of flamingos, the

Slimbridge is home to over 160 different types of wildfowl.

white winged wood duck – which is probably the rarest duck in the world – and a Tropical House where birds such as humming birds fly free amongst vines and orchids. Many of the residents were once threatened with extinction before the trust was formed.

The site has observation towers that afford excellent views across the Severn estuary, has a large free car park and is open every day from 9.30-4.30.

BERKELEY CASTLE Gloucestershire

For over 800 years Berkeley Castle has been home to the Berkeley family, but the residence of the family has not been without drama. In 1215 the castle was the meeting place for the barons prior to witnessing the Magna Carta, and in 1327 Edward II was imprisoned for five months until he was eventually tortured to death by his jailers. Present-day visitors can view the murder room, and the pit down which rotting carcasses were thrown.

Although a castle with buttresses and battlements, it is more a home than a fortress. It is built of sandstone and pale grey puffstone on which grows wisteria. Much of the building is open to the public.

There is a picture gallery incorporating paintings by Van de Velde, a dining room, and a kitchen containing a magnificent solid oak table which is almost two feet thick, a spit, original lead sinks, and larders that are tiled both on the ground and walls for coolness and hung with huge meat hooks. The two drawing rooms contain 18th-century gilded furniture much of which has been embroidered with the Berkeley crest by successive Lady Berkeley's, and there is also some ebony furniture which is said to have originated from Drake's ship. The Great Hall is enormous and has a ceiling rising to over 30 feet which is supported by huge arched timbers.

Berkeley Castle (opposite page).

The castle is set in terraced gardens created this century by Captain R G Berkeley, and a deer park. There is also an Elizabethan garden and a bowling green. Next to the castle is the parish church of St Mary the Virgin where physician Edward Jenner, the inventor of the smallpox vaccine, is buried.

DROITWICH SPA BRINE BATH
Hereford & Worcester

The Romans first discovered the extensive bed of rock salt lying beneath Droitwich and this natural resource created great wealth for the area, but it was not until a later date that the Droitwich Spa Brine Baths were built. John Corbett conceived the idea of the baths in the early 19th century in response to the Victorian demand for a fashionable and healthy resort. The waters are ten times more salty than sea water and are said to be even more salty than the Dead Sea. They are relaxing as well as soothing for rheumatism and the salt makes the body so weightless that even the poorest swimmer will find floating in the water relatively easy.

Recently the spa has enjoyed a revival in popularity, and the baths were refurbished and a new brine bath opened in the 1980s. The new bath has clean and filtered water pumped into a pool kept at 33°C. The baths also include other fitness and health facilities and are open by appointment only, all year round.

During his lifetime the instigator of the baths, John Corbett, established many luxury hotels in the area. He built a French château, now the Château Impney Hotel, set in a 70-acre estate, which stands nearby at Dodderhill.

SEVERN VALLEY RAILWAY

During the late 19th century the Severn Valley Railway was part of the Great Western Railway line. In 1965 the line, which was then disused, was destined to be demolished but was saved by the Severn Valley Railway Society. After renovation the line was re-opened in 1970 and initially trains ran from Bridgnorth to Bewdley, but in 1984 the line was extended to Kidderminster. Today the standard gauge line is excellently preserved and the steam engine takes passengers along a sixteen mile stretch which roughly follows the River Severn, sometimes by clinging to the valley sides and at others by running parallel to the River Severn.

The line passes the West Midland Safari Park, through agricultural lands where sheep graze on the hillside and past the heathland of the Wyre Forest.

The train runs through stations at Arley, Highley, Hampton Loade and Bewdley – where there is a carriage and wagon workshop and a model railway. Just past Bewdley the train crosses the river on the Victoria Bridge, built in 1861, which at 200 feet was then the world's largest cast iron span.

Visitors to the Wedgwood Centre can see pot-throwing and turning on the lathe in progress.

The station at Kidderminster is a step back to Victoriana, with old posters advertising popular seaside trips, old leather suitcases and the red fire buckets of the Great Western Railway. At the other end of the line Bridgnorth is the main locomotive depot for the society, and here visitors can see Britain's largest working collection of standard gauge steam and diesel locomotives including passenger steam engines, industrial and diesel locomotives which are occasionally fuelled for action during enthusiasts' weekends.

The stations are open daily, but the trains run only from mid-May to the end of September.

WEDGWOOD VISITOR CENTRE
near Stoke-on-Trent, Staffordshire

The Wedgwood Visitor Centre is set in 550 acres of parkland four miles south of Stoke-on-Trent. The centre contains an extensive collection of Wedgwood which dates from 1759 when Wedgwood first opened his factory at Burslem, to the present day.

As well as a potter, from a family of potters, Wedgwood was a writer, industrialist

and scientist and he invented the pyrometer for measuring extreme heat, but it is for his unique pottery that we remember him. Today visitors can see the Jasperware – the white figurines on a blue blackground – which gained him fame and which visitors to the centre can see being made by craftsmen.

Other exhibits include an 18th-century first edition Portland Vase, and a black basalt vase made by Josiah Wedgwood himself to commemorate the opening of his new factory in Etruria, where he built a village for his workers in 1789. Today the industry he began is one of the largest in the world.

The Wedgwood Centre also includes an art gallery and a display of crafts which are demonstrated in the hall. These include pot-throwing, turning on the lathe, and the intricate work of forming classical ornaments.

The centre is open daily all year round except Sundays.

The Wedgwood Visitor Centre contains an extensive collection of Wedgwood dating from 1759.

STRATFORD-UPON-AVON
Warwickshire

Stratford-upon-Avon is famous as the birth-place in 1564 of William Shakespeare and today the town is full of reminders of his former presence. Visitors can view the most notable points of Shakespearean interest during guided tours in open top buses which run every fifteen minutes.

Places with Shakespearean interest include the Royal Shakespeare Theatre Picture Gallery which contains portraits, original costumes and design sets from Shakespeare's productions from 1879 to 1968; Wilmcote, the home of Shakespeare's mother; Hall Croft, the home of his daughter and her husband Dr John Hall; and the family home of Shakespeare's parents which has been restored and furnished in the style of the period. Only the foundations of Shakespeare's own house remain, and these form part of the garden of Nash's House, which is now a museum.

The town is still a literary centre; the Royal Shakespeare Theatre, first opened in 1932, performs mainly Shakespeare plays. Every summer there is a drama festival which was first established by actor David Garrick in 1769. The most noted productions from this festival usually proceed to London.

As well as William Shakespeare, many other famous names are linked to the town, such as John Harvard – founder of the famous University – whose grandparents once lived at Harvard House; and Hugh Clopton, a benefactor of the town who built the fourteen arched Clopton Bridge and later became Lord Mayor of London. Other famous visitors to the town were author Sir Walter Scott, and actor Henry Irving.

The heart of Stratford is still true to its medieval pattern, with streets running parallel and at right angles to the river. Many of the half-timbered and thatched houses are

Knott Garden, New Place, Stratford-upon-Avon.

Stratford-upon-Avon is inextricably linked to Shakespeare, who was born there. His birthplace (above, left, and right) is open to the public. The home of Mary Arden (top), his mother, is perhaps the least familiar of the houses associated with the playwright.

gone, but some remain together with some Georgian red brick buildings to give a nostalgic reminder of past eras.

Other places of interest include the Butterfly and Jungle Safari, which is Europe's largest live butterfly safari. Here visitors can view tarantulas, scorpions and the world's largest spider. There is also a Motor Museum, housed in a former church, dis-

playing Rolls Royces, Bugattis and Lagondas. In the summer house of the Royal Shakespeare Theatre can be found a unique collection of brass rubbings of knights, courtiers, and kings of the Shakespearean era.

It is hardly surprising Stratford is rated second only to London as Britain's largest tourist town.

The Royal Shakespeare Theatre, Stratford – home to a unique collection of brass rubbings as well as The Royal Shakespeare Company.

FOR FURTHER INFORMATION CONTACT:

Tourist Information Centre
St Michael's Tower
The Cross
CIRENCESTER
Gloucestershire
GL1 1PD
Telephone: (0452) 421188

Tourist Information Centre
Judith Shakespeare's House
1 High Street
STRATFORD-UPON-AVON
Warwickshire
CV37 6AU
Telephone: (0789) 293127/67522

Tourist Information Centre
Guildhall
High Street
WORCESTER
Worcestershire
WR1 2EX
Telephone: (0905) 723471 Ext. 201

Heart of England Tourist Board
2/4 Trinity Street
WORCESTER
Worcestershire
WR1 2PW
Telephone: (0905) 613132

WALES

In the Pennant Valley.

Wales is an area of outstanding natural beauty and consists of many acres of national parkland. The largest of these is the Snowdonian National Park which dominates the north. The area has an ever changing vista of mountain forests rising to bare crags, lakes, valleys, and thundering waterfalls. There are roads clinging to sheer mountain sides which lead to tiny village settlements where inhabitants still converse in native Welsh.

Many castles were built in the area and these include Conway, built by Edward I during his battle with the Welsh Prince Llewelyn. The castle provides a perfect vantage point to see the ancient craftsmanship of the three bridges spanning the river Conway. Indeed there are many bridges dotted around the countryside. The most famous is the Menai Bridge spanning the Menai Strait which joins the Isle of Anglesey – with its 125 miles of coastline – to the northern mainland.

Offering a sharp contrast to the bustle of Conway are the depths of rural North Wales. The vale of Ffestiniog, for example, is a slate quarrying district of isolated villages and vast stretches of chill grey rock.

Further south and set against the backcloth of the Cambrian mountains is the beautiful coastline and sparsely populated sheep rearing country of mid Wales. In the nothern half the beaches are backed by sand dunes and in the south are overlooked by gorse covered cliffs. For centuries the area has been famous for spa waters, and many of these towns have become inland resorts.

South Wales is another area dotted with national parks. These include the grassy mountains and moorland of the Brecon Beacons, the sandy coves of the Gower peninsula, the hills of the Wye Valley, the tiny thatched cottages and fields of the Heritage Coast of the Vale of Glamorgan and the bays of the Pembrokeshire Coast National Park.

Inland historic places of interest include the Preseli Mountains (from which the blue stones of Stonehenge came), Laugharne Castle once painted by Turner, and Laugharne Church – burial place of Dylan Thomas.

Wales is the home of cheeses, and as a fishing area there are a great deal of locally caught delicacies to sample. It is also an area of home baking, and visitors should look out for locally made cheesecake and welsh pancakes.

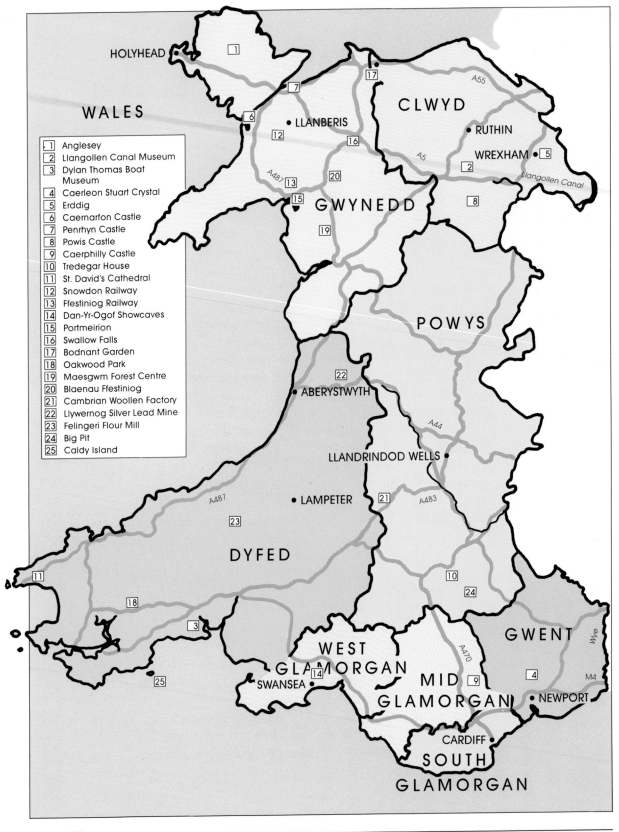

WALES

HOLYHEAD

1 Anglesey

CLWYD

7

17

A55

6

12 LLANBERIS

RUTHIN

16

A5

WREXHAM

2

5

A487 13

20

Llangollen Canal

15

GWYNEDD

8

19

1 Anglesey
2 Llangollen Canal Museum
3 Dylan Thomas Boat Museum
4 Caerleon Stuart Crystal
5 Erddig
6 Caernarfon Castle
7 Penrhyn Castle
8 Powis Castle
9 Caerphilly Castle
10 Tredegar House
11 St. David's Cathedral
12 Snowdon Railway
13 Ffestiniog Railway
14 Dan-Yr-Ogof Showcaves
15 Portmeirion
16 Swallow Falls
17 Bodnant Garden
18 Oakwood Park
19 Maesgwm Forest Centre
20 Blaenau Ffestiniog
21 Cambrian Woollen Factory
22 Llywernog Silver Lead Mine
23 Felingeri Flour Mill
24 Big Pit
25 Caldy Island

POWYS

22

ABERYSTWYTH

A44

LLANDRINDOD WELLS

LAMPETER

21

A483

23

DYFED

11

10

18

24

3

GWENT

Wye

25

WEST GLAMORGAN

14

MID GLAMORGAN

A470

9

4

M4

SWANSEA

NEWPORT

CARDIFF

SOUTH GLAMORGAN

Ffestiniog Railway Gwynedd

Slate from the huge quarries at Blaenau Ffestiniog used to be carried to the coast by rail to be exported from Porthmadog. The narrow-gauge line, which originally opened in 1836, closed almost 100 years later, but restoration work began in 1954 and now trains run along it again.

From the coast at Porthmadog, the little trains climb through the Snowdonia National Park with its peaceful pastures and magnificent forest, past lakes and waterfalls, to Blaenau Ffestiniog, 700 feet above sea-level. Sometimes they stop at isolated cottages whose inhabitants are completely dependent on the railway for transport. Many of the trains undertaking the 13½-mile, one-hour journey are hauled by historic steam locomotives, some of which have served the line for over 100 years.

Trains run daily from the end of March to the end of October, and their frequency depends on the time of year. There is a limited winter service. Passengers can leave the train at any of the stations along the route to visit places of interest like Llechwedd Slate Caverns and the Gloddfa Ganol Slate Mine (Blaenau Ffestiniog), the Ffestiniog Power Station (Tanygrisiau) where there is a visitor centre and guided tours, and Portmeirion. Scenic walks start from the stations at Tan-y-Bwlch and Dduallt.

A hanging basket adorns Porthmadog station (above) where the historic steam trains leave for Snowdonia (right).

ISLE OF ANGLESEY

Just off the coast of north Wales, the Isle of Anglesey is fast becoming a holiday destination in its own right. Its unspoilt and varied scenery makes it an ideal centre for walking, riding or sailing, and it is a stronghold of the Welsh language and culture.

Wildlife thrives, thanks to the island's mild maritime climate and varied habitats. The cliff walks at Ynys Llanddwyn are carpeted with bluebells in spring; visitors to South Stack in their May and June breeding seasons include huge numbers of guillemots, razorbills and puffins; autumn brings the changing colours of turning leaves and berried hedgerows; while just over the Menai Straits on the mainland the dramatic snow-covered mountains of Snowdonia dominate the winter landscape.

Among the man-made attractions are Beaumaris Castle, where summer-time entertainment includes medieval music, tournaments, jugglers and fire-eaters. There is a butterfly farm at Pili-Palas near the Menai Bridge, and the Sea Zoo at Bryn-siencyn offers visitors the chance to explore underwater habitats and wildlife without ever getting wet.

Those in search of Anglesey's history find it at the ancient monument of Bryn-Celli-Dhu, the best example of an ancient passage-grave in Britain, and Din Lligwy, where the remains of a pre-Roman settlement were discovered. The more recent past is preserved at Plas Newydd, the imposing home of the Marquesses of Anglesey, now in the care of the National Trust.

Not far from Plas Newydd is the village boasting one of the longest names ever, a concoction apparently dreamed up by a local 19th-century businessman. Nobody seriously expects a non Welsh-speaker to be able to pronounce Llanfairpwllgwyngyllgogerychwyrndrobwllllantysiliogogogoch

Looking out onto the unspoilt scenery of Anglesey from Mynedd.

The Isle of Anglesey offers a host of attractions, from the Anglesey Sea Zoo (top left and right) to the moated castle (above) and fascinating Museum of Childhood (right) at Beaumaris.

(which means 'St Mary's by the white aspen over the whirlpool and St Tysilio's by the red cave'), but many try. The village's tourist centre houses displays covering Anglesey's geology, history and local features.

BLAENAU FFESTINIOG *Gwynedd*

At the head of the beautiful Vale of Ffestiniog is the mountain town of Blaenau Ffestiniog, surrounded by the majestic Meolwyn and Manod mountain ranges. Until the start of the 20th century, when other roofing materials became more popular, this was an important slate-quarrying area; now tourists can travel as the miners once did to explore the region's industrial heritage.

Visitors can explore the region's industrial heritage at Gloddfa Ganol Slate Mine.

At Llechwedd Slate Caverns, visitors can actually go underground to see the former slate workings. On the surface, the Slate Heritage Theatre is the venue for a 25-minute programme illustrating the story of the Welsh slate industry since Roman times; rolling stock and other equipment from the four rival railways which once competed for Blaenau Ffestiniog's slate-carrying trade are on display. Slate souvenirs are made and sold here.

North of the town is the Gloddfa Ganol Mountain Tourist Centre, created on a mountain of slate out of a quarry's former buildings and some of its 42 miles of tunnels. As well as a museum and gallery, there are walks with panoramic views; visitors can also try their hand at splitting slate.

As it was at the height of its prosperity, Blaenau Ffestiniog is still the starting-point of the narrow-gauge Ffestiniog Railway which once carried slate from the mountains to Porthmadog for export.

Reminders of the area's former industrial importance include the Conwy Valley Railways Museum, sited in what was once the old goods yard by the railway station; Thomas Telford's iron Waterloo Bridge across the Conwy; and the former lead-mining centre at Cyffty in Gwydyr Forest, where visitors can explore the old mine buildings.

BODNANT GARDEN
Near Colwyn Bay, Gwynedd

Though a relatively new garden, Bodnant is widely considered to be one of the finest in the world. Its 80 acres are situated on south-west-sloping ground above the River Conway, and look over the river valley towards Snowdonia.

Successive Lords Aberconway have superintended the garden's development since it was begun by the family in 1875, and continue to do so though Bodnant has been in the care of the National Trust since 1949. Skilful planting means that there are

spectacular displays in both formal and informal settings between mid-March and the end of October, which is when the garden is open to the public.

Spring bulbs make an appearance at the beginning of the season, followed by masses of rhododendrons, magnolias and camellias which bloom until the end of June. Towards the end of May the famous Laburnam Arch comes into flower; elsewhere azaleas make a colourful show. The herbaceous borders, roses, water lilies, clematis and other wall-climbers make the Terrace Gardens the place

to be during the summer months; eucryphias and hydrangeas are the main attraction during August and September. October sees the garden taking on its autumn colouring.

Many of the plants on view in the garden are propagated at the garden's own nursery, and on sale to the public. They include over 800 species and varieties of flowering and foliage shrubs — including rhododendrons, azaleas, magnolias and camellias — though not all are available for purchase all the time. Bodnant's nursery and plant centre are open all year.

Laburnum Arch at Bodnant Garden.

CAERNARFON CASTLE Gwynedd

It took 37 years to build Caernarfon Castle from the time when it was commissioned by Edward I as a symbol of English power in Wales. One of Europe's great medieval fortresses, the castle has been owned by the English monarchs ever since its foundation in 1283 and still plays an important part in the life of the 20th-century Royal Family.

The present Queen's son, Charles, was created Prince of Wales here in 1969, as George V's son had been 60 years earlier. Over the years, ruling monarchs have used it as a base for visiting the Principality.

Caernarfon Castle is one of the most popular visitor attractions in Wales. Its imposing walls were modelled on those surrounding the ancient city of Constantinople, while its King's Gate has been described as the mightiest in the land. The Eagle Tower now houses an exhibition and audiovisual programme, the Queen's Tower is home to the regimental museum of the Royal Welsh Fusiliers, and situated in the Chamberlain Tower is an exhibition featuring King Edward I's castles.

Ideal as a base for touring the Snowdonia National Park and the island of Anglesey, the town of Caernarfon is also an important shopping centre. A Saturday market is held on the Square in front of the castle. Leisure amenities include an art gallery, two yacht clubs, tennis, golf and bowls facilities, while sea- and river-fishing opportunities are said to be among the finest in Britain.

Caernarfon Castle (opposite page and below) is one of Europe's great medieval fortresses, its walls modelled on those of Constantinople.

The village of Portmeirion, a unique architectural work of art (opposite page).

RUTHIN Clwyd

Every evening at eight o'clock, the curfew bell tolls in Ruthin as it has done since the 11th century. An important market town since medieval times, Ruthin's historic buildings include what is left of the 13th-century castle around which the fortified town originally grew up, and which are some of the oldest such remains in Wales. In the 19th century, a Gothic-style castle was grafted onto the original building, and is now a luxury hotel.

Medieval days are held regularly in Ruthin throughout the summer, and evidence of Ruthin's medieval heritage survives in the shape of St Peter's Church, with its carved oak roof, and the half-timbered Old Courthouse (now a bank) with fine woodwork inside and part of its original gallows still visible on an outside wall. Another bank now occupies 16th-century Exmewe Hall, outside which is Maen Huail (Huail's Stone) on which King Arthur is said to have had a rival in love beheaded.

The spectacular cascading Swallow Falls.

Ruthin has been a market town and craft centre since its early days, and the tradition has continued in the 20th century with the opening of a purpose-built craft centre on the site of the old railway station. Each of fourteen independent units houses its own workshops where craftsmen produce a variety of goods. Visitors are welcome to watch the craftsmen at work, and to buy.

Picturesquely located in the Vale of Clwyd, Ruthin enjoys easy access to many beauty-spots. There are marked footpaths on the surrounding hills, and country parks and isolated villages to explore. Local sporting facilities include golf, tennis, swimming (Ruthin has an indoor pool), cricket, football, rugby, fishing and pony trekking.

SWALLOW FALLS Betws-y-Coed, Gwynedd

Three rivers – the Conwy, Llugwy and Lledr – meet at Betsw-y-Coed, a popular touring centre since Victorian times. Surrounded by the Gwydyr Forest, and well served by hotels and guest-houses, the town is a renowned beauty-spot in its own right as well as being an ideal centre from which to explore north Wales.

Betws-y-Coed's most famous sight is the Swallow Falls, two miles out of town, where a railed footpath provides access to spectacular views of the cascading river-waters as they tumble down their wooded gorge. Also worth a visit are the nearby Conwy Falls, where a man-made salmon leap helps the fish reach their up-river spawning grounds, and a nature trail passes through unspoilt deciduous woodland.

In the town itself is the 15th-century Pont-y-Pair (Bridge of the Cauldron) across the River Llugwy.

PORTMEIRION Gwynedd

In 1925 the rocky promontory on which Portmeirion stands was an abandoned wilderness accessible only from the sea. Architect Sir Clough Williams-Ellis acquired the land to build a village and prove that man-made structures could enhance the landscape rather than defile it.

Portmeirion, with its graceful, pastel-coloured buildings, elegant bell-tower and central square, was inspired by the Italian

fishing village of Portofino. Designed to be self-supporting right from the start, it grew around an old house already on the shore, which was opened as a hotel in 1926. Cottages were constructed around this nucleus, and became part of the hotel's accommodation; other buildings were added for visual impact.

Set within woods and farmland, Portmeirion now has around a quarter of a million visitors a year, attracted by the natural beauty of the area in which it stands as well as the village's own charms. Accommodation is available at the hotel or in one of its associated self-catering cottages; day visitors, welcome between Easter and October, pay an entrance charge.

CANAL MUSEUM Llangollen, Clwyd

Vitally important to Britain's industrial development in the 18th and 19th centuries, the canal network – all 5000 miles of it –

At the Llangollen Canal Exhibition Centre visitors can find out about the working and recreational uses of canals.

carried coal in large quantities from mining areas to the factories which depended on it. Llangollen's Canal Museum tells the story of how the canals which made up that network were built, how they handled and carried their cargo, the methods that were used to get them up and down mountains, and the ways in which they contributed to Britain's Industrial Revolution.

Other exhibits cover the people who worked this great transport system, and bring the story to contemporary times with studies of the present-day importance of the canals as recreational centres and habitats for wildlife. The museum, on Llangollen Wharf, is open every day from Easter until the end of September.

Horse-drawn passenger-boats leave Llangollen Wharf several times a day between the months of April and October, giving visitors a first-hand opportunity to explore the section of canal that runs through the beautiful Vale of Llangollen; longer trips cater for booked parties of 35 or more people.

ERDDIG Near Wrexham

Built in the 1680s, and home of a single family of country squires from 1753 to 1973, Erddig has remained relatively undisturbed for centuries.

Early occupants with an eye for beautiful things furnished Erddig in magnificent style; later ones cherished everything, added their own pieces, and threw nothing away. Tapestries, oriental porcelain, silver, early 18th-century furniture (much still with its original upholstery), mirrors and paintings are all on view.

Erddig is more, however, than a monument to generations of collectors. Such a country house could not have been run without its staff and the network of support services they maintained: clear evidence of their presence remains in the shape of the estate's smithy, joiner's shop, sawpit, laundries, bakehouse and kitchens – all still much the same as they were in Erddig's heyday.

Erdigg has remained relatively undisturbed for centuries.

Likenesses of generations of family servants in the form of paintings, daguerrotypes and photographs commemorate their contribution, going right back to the 18th-century house carpenter, spider-brusher and gamekeeper.

Outside, Erddig's gardens are essentially the same as they were in 1740. Restorations and replantings have preserved the bones of the original Dutch-style garden layout, with its formal walks, canal, pond and lime avenue. The fine landscaped park is complete with a striking circular waterfall.

Erddig is open between Easter and late October, though times and days vary throughout the season. Guided tours – one taking in 'below stairs' and the estate outbuildings, another adding the family rooms – are available.

Rock Park Spa
Llandrindod Wells, Powys

When gout was a fashionable complaint in Victorian and Edwardian times, Llandrindod Wells was in its heyday. The healing qualities associated with the town's mineral waters had first become famous in the reign of Charles II and, by the mid-19th century, 80,000 visitors a year made it the most popular of the Welsh spas.

The broad streets and Georgian-style architecture of Llandrindod Wells recall a more leisurely time when 'taking the waters' had royal approval and was very definitely the thing to do. Spacious parks, quiet walks and capacious hotels still remain as a permanent legacy of those prosperous days.

Today the town is the administrative centre for Powys and one of Wales's most popular inland resorts, and it is still possible to sample the waters on which its reputation rests.

Rock Park Pump Room was built in 1867, but 100 years later it had fallen into disuse and disrepair. Now renovated by Radnor District Council and the Wales Tourist Board to house an exhibition hall, visitor centre

The 19th-century Penrhyn Castle (opposite page) is built of stone from Anglesey.

and tea room, it once contained medicinal baths and treatment rooms.

Today's visitors can taste the sulphur- and saline-rich waters by the glass, or sample chalybeate water direct from its spring. Chalybeate water was said to be a useful tonic, and was recommended at the end of the 19th century for anaemia and general debility, but it was sulphur's health-giving properties which seem to have appealed to the Victorians. Either on its own or with saline water, it was thought to be efficacious in the treatment of everything from eczema to rheumatism – including gout.

Penrhyn Castle
Near Bangor, Gwynedd

Although Penrhyn Castle looks Norman, it was actually the work of Thomas Hopper, who conceived it early in the 19th century for the immensely wealthy owner of the Penrhyn slate quarries. Hopper was also given a free hand with the interior decoration and the design of much of the castle's furniture.

Penrhyn is built of local stone from Anglesey, and its elaborately ornate interior makes much use of the slate on which its owner's wealth depended. Some people think the curious mixture of styles which characterises Hopper's work at Penrhyn leads to a whole which is architecturally right over the top: the National Trust, which now manages the property, suggests that it is most likely to appeal to those with what it calls a robust architectural digestion.

Standing in extensive grounds between mountains and sea, the castle (open to the public between the beginning of April and early November) is home to a selection of the 1st Lord Penrhyn's old master paintings and the National Trust's fine collection of over 800 dolls. Also here, in Hopper's vast stables, is an important museum of industrial locomotives, complete with full-size engines and rolling-stock from the great slate quarries of the area.

LLANBERIS Gwynedd

At the foot of Snowdon, and more than 3000 feet below its summit, is the little town of Llanberis. The easiest walk (3½ miles) to the top of the mountain starts here, as does the hour long, 4½-mile trip aboard the only rack and pinion steam railway in Britain.

Weather permitting, trains run on the Snowdon Mountain Railway most days between mid-March and the end of October (every day during June, July and August), though times vary according to demand.

Down in the valley, another narrow-gauge line (Llanberis Lake Railway) runs alongside Llyn Padarn. The huge quarries served by the line were once the world's greatest, but were closed in 1969 because of the slump in demand for the material they produced. The Welsh Slate Centre, within the Padarn Country Park, is open from Easter to September and contains much original machinery from the quarry's workshops, together with the 54-foot waterwheel that used to power it. The lakeside meadows and woodland that border Llyn Padarn are popular walking and picnic areas; dinghies are available for hire from the spring bank holiday until the end of September.

Overlooking the valley south of Llanberis are the ruins of Dolbadarn Castle, with its three-storey, 13th-century round tower. Opposite the castle, across the lake (Llyn Peris), is the largest pumped-storage power station in Europe, most of which is buried in man-made caverns deep within Elidir Fawr mountain. Its visitor centre is open daily between Easter and the end of October. Guided underground tours of the hydro-electric power station can be arranged for organised groups, but must be booked in advance.

The beautiful countryside around Llanberis makes the town a popular centre for climbing, walking and watersports. Annual events based at the town include its Carnival

The Snowdon Mountain Railway.

(July), the internationally known Snowdon Mountain Race (to the mountain's summit and back on Carnival Day, the third Saturday in July), and the Llyn Padarn Swim along the length of the lake (fourth Saturday in July). The Snowdon Marathon attracts runners from all over Britain on the last Sunday in October.

VALE OF RHEIDOL RAILWAY
From Aberystwyth, Dyfed

British Rail's last remaining steam engines regularly climb the twelve miles from Aberystwyth through spectacular woodland scenery to the mountain terminus of Devil's Bridge. Opened in 1902 to carry ore from the lead mines in the Rheidol Valley, the 1' 11½"-gauge line was soon popular with tourists attracted by Devil's Bridge's plunging gorges and wooded chasms, nearly 700 feet above sea level.

For the first few miles, the track follows the valley floor before hugging forested hillsides further into its hour-long route. As it climbs, it clings to a narrow ledge high above the valley – it was the nature of this kind of terrain which originally dictated the width of the track. Though the lines on which they travel are on an unusually small scale, there is nothing puny about the Rheidol Railway's three locomotives, which are more than eight feet wide and weigh in at over 25 tons.

Trains run between Easter and spring bank holiday, then from early June to the beginning of October. There is plenty of time between trains at Devil's Bridge to explore some of the stunning sights nearby, which include the Mynach Falls, the Devil's Punchbowl and Jacob's Ladder.

THE CAMBRIAN FACTORY
Llanwrtyd Wells, Powys

Weavers have been plying their trade in Wales for at least 500 years, producing cloth in unique patterns and colours from the wool of the sheep who graze the country's hillsides and pastures. It is a tradition that continues today, and visitors can see the various processes which transform raw wool into the finest Welsh Tweed as they happen at the Cambrian Factory.

Sorting, dyeing, carding, spinning, winding and weaving all take place here, and the end products – either in the form of knitting yard or lengths of tweed fabrics – are on sale along with finished items in the factory's shop.

Easily accessible, and situated in some lovely countryside, the Cambrian Factory was established by the British Legion in 1918 to give employment to ex-Service personnel disabled in World War One. Over the years, other disabled people have joined the staff.

The factory is open on weekdays all year, except on bank holidays and over Christmas; the shop from Monday to Saturday (closed Saturday afternoons from October to April), including bank holidays but not Christmas.

ABERYSTWYTH Dyfed

Aberystwyth's delightful hotel-lined seafront promenade.

Located on a prehistoric site at the mouths of the rivers Rheidol and Ystwyth, 20th-century Aberystwyth is a seaside resort, university town and the main administrative centre for the Cardigan Bay coast. It has been important since the 13th century, when a castle was first built there; later destroyed by Cromwell's forces, its remains are still on the seafront, with public gardens now laid out in what were once its precincts.

Opposite is the Victorian Gothic building which is the nucleus of the University of Wales, whose campus on Penglais Hill includes the National Library of Wales. Within the Library is the finest collection anywhere of Welsh manuscripts and books, as well as maps, prints and portraits with Welsh connections.

Aberystwyth's lively, hotel-lined seafront promenade borders a beach of fine gravel and shingle. Here are traditional resort attractions for children like a paddling pool, trampolines, donkey rides and boat trips. From the northern end of the promenade, the longest electric cliff railway in Britain climbs to the summit of Constitution Hill and the Great Aberystwyth Camera Obscura, one of the novelties – like the funicular railway – that made the town so attractive to Victorian holiday-makers.

Entertainment during the summer months includes drama on the beach, and concerts and evening shows on the promenade. On the University campus is the

Aberystwyth Arts Centre which incorporates a concert hall, the university theatre where plays are produced throughout the holiday season, and an art gallery.

Within easy reach of the resort are facilities for all kinds of sports including sea fishing, golf, tennis and bowls. The Vale of Rheidol narrow-gauge railway operates from Aberystwyth's Alexandra Road Station, and Llywernog Silver Lead Mine is not far away.

LLYWERNOG SILVER LEAD MINE
Ponterwyd, Dyfed

In the mountains ten miles east of Aberystwyth, and housed in what used to be its mine buildings, the Llywernog Silver Lead Mine exhibition is open to visitors every day from Easter to October.

Though parts of the site are still awaiting restoration, the mine's main building now houses re-creations of underground scenes and the 'California of Wales' mining exhibition.

Various items of original equipment can be seen like the giant waterwheels which generated power for the mine, and the marked Miners' Trail actually takes visitors into the mountain before directing them to other points of interest on the site.

This is only one of a number of trails introducing visitors to the industrial archaeology of mid Wales: details of others are featured in *A Glimpse of the Past*, available from Wales Tourist Board.

FELIN GERI MILL
Near Newcastle Emlyn, Dyfed

Open to the public between Easter and October, the 16th-century watermill at Felin Geri continues to produce the stone-ground wholemeal flour that has made it famous. One of the last commercially operated watermills in the country, it is now the centrepiece of a complex which includes amongst its

The giant waterwheel at Llywernog Silver Lead Mine.

attractions a small museum of rural life, a rare collection of antique angling equipment and a giant adventure playground.

Nature trails through the countryside nearby are introduced by exhibits at a Woodland Interpretation Centre, manned by members of Dyfed Wildlife Trust whose job is to guide visitors to the wildlife of the beautiful Ceri Valley. A network of farm paths over twelve acres of hillside gives access to part of the valley which has been left untouched for hundreds of years.

Felin Geri's licensed restaurant, housed in the buildings where wood ovens used to dry green grain, is open every day during the summer season.

The romantic Powis Castle has been inhabited continually for five centuries.

POWIS CASTLE *Near Welshpool, Powys*

Unlike most of the other great 13th-century fortresses in Wales, Powis Castle has never been allowed to fall into ruin. One of the most romantic of the castles that once guarded the Welsh Marches, it has been the ancestral home of the Herbert family since 1587 and inhabited continuously for over five centuries. Alterations dating from the end of the 16th century reflect the castle's changing role from fortress to family house, and successive generations have continued to adapt it to suit their needs, so the interior is a rich mixture of styles and periods.

Changing tastes in interior decoration have left their mark. The long gallery is Elizabethan, while the state bedroom dates from the time of Charles II. The Great Staircase, painted with murals by Lanscroon, is signed and dated 1705, the Blue Drawing Room is Georgian in character, and the Oak Drawing Room reflects the trends of the early 20th century. Fine furniture is on display throughout.

Also on display is the Clive of India collection of treasure from the subcontinent, which arrived at Powis via a Herbert heiress who married the son of Clive of India.

Powis's magnificent gardens are thought to date from the 17th century. With their strong sense of order, they are typical of their time – and, unlike many other gardens of the period, were not swept away by the passion for more natural landscapes associated with Capability Brown. Four richly-planted terraces, each around 200 yards long, are set on the steep slope below the castle. From them is a fine view across to wide, level lawns and wooded hillsides.

Castle and garden are open between the end of March and early November, though days and times vary with the season. On Sunday afternoons during the winter months only the gardens, Clive Museum and tea rooms are open to the public.

MAESGWM FOREST VISITOR CENTRE
Near Dolgellau, Gwynedd

Throughout the glorious countryside of mid Wales, various official bodies – park authorities, the Forestry Commission and the Nature Conservancy Council among them – have created nature and forest trails which give visitors a real feeling for their surroundings. Maesgwm Forest Visitor Centre was one of the first of its kind to be established in Wales, and is one of a series in this part of the country.

Surrounded by a network of walks through the Brenin Forest, the Visitor Centre mounts a series of exhibits designed to interpret the area in order to add to walkers' enjoyment and understanding of the region as a whole. Surface features are traced back to their underlying geology; soils and natural forest vegetation are described. Man's impact on the forest, and the ways in which changing patterns of land use have affected the environment, are illustrated, as are the various functions of today's man-made woodland.

The Visitor Centre is open from Monday to Saturday between Easter and October.

ST DAVID'S CATHEDRAL AND BISHOP'S PALACE St David's, Dyfed

The tiny city of St David's bears the name of the patron saint of Wales who established a centre of Christianity here in the 6th century. Its 12th-century cathedral, the third to have been built on the same spot, was not actually finished until 1572. Built of purple-coloured stone, some of which was quarried from nearby Caerbwdi, the cathedral occupies a shallow vale, out of sight of early marauders, and has been a place of pilgrimage for centuries.

Though its exterior is plain, the cathedral's interior has some superb decoration including ornate carvings on the choir stalls, a fine Irish oak roof in the nave, and delicate fan vaulting above the Holy Trinity Chapel. Relics of St David lie in an inner sanctuary behind the high altar.

Not far away, across a brook, are the ruins of the Bishop's Palace, built by one bishop in 1340 and destroyed by another in the 15th century. What is left of its battlements, curtain walls and gatehouse speak of a troubled time when even churchmen felt a need for fortifications. Decorated with some of the

St David's Cathedral has long been a place of pilgrimage.

finest sculptured heads and animal figures in Wales, a 14th-century parapet extends along both main wings of the palace; the remains of other elaborate decorative features still remain.

Life in a medieval bishop's household is the subject of an exhibition in the palace, which includes a model of the building as it was before its destruction.

THE BOATHOUSE Laugharne, Dyfed

Poet Dylan Thomas lived for a time in the Georgian boathouse on the banks of the River Taf which is now a museum dedicated to his life and work. Though there is some doubt that *Under Milk Wood*, the drama for which he is probably best known, was set in Laugharne, it does recapture some of the atmosphere of this quaint village with its Georgian terraced streets and old harbour.

Brown's Hotel was one of Thomas's favourite watering-holes, and he is buried in Laugharne churchyard.

CAERLEON Near Newport, Gwent

Isca, along with Chester and York, one of the principal military bases in Roman Britain, was headquarters of the 5,600-man Second Augustinian Legion which spearheaded the final Roman advance into south Wales. The remains of this legionary fortress – the only ones on view anywhere in Europe – bring many visitors to Caerleon.

Each barrack building was once home to 80 men and their centurian. Visitors can walk along a Roman street and discover the remains of their turrets, cookhouses and bread ovens – even their toilet facilities. The soldiers' main leisure centre – the Fortress Baths, whose concrete vaults once stood 60 feet high – was discovered as recently as 1964; artists' reconstructions, a spoken commentary and computer graphics help re-create them for today's visitors.

Just outside the fortress walls stands the Roman Amphitheatre, designed to seat 5000

Caerphilly Castle (opposite page) has its own Leaning Tower of Pisa, a result of an attack by Cromwellian troops.

spectators. It continues to provide a spectacular setting for festivals, though the gladiatorial combats and animal-baiting that took place there in Roman times have long since gone.

Exhibitions in the new Legionary Museum, a branch gallery of the National Museum of Wales, illustrate the history of Roman Caerleon and the daily life of the garrison.

CAERPHILLY CASTLE
Caerphilly, Mid Glamorgan

One of the greatest surviving medieval castles of the western world, Caerphilly was virtually impregnable against the siege methods used at the time when it was built.

Completed in 1270, the castle's massive gatehouses, water defences and huge curtain walls rendered it almost invulnerable for around 500 years. Only when attacked by Cromwellian troops in the 17th century did it show any sign of weakness, and evidence of their onslaught remains today in the shape of a ruined round tower that leans even further off the vertical than the Leaning Tower of Pisa.

It is not difficult to see why Caerphilly Castle presented such an obstacle to those who threatened it. The 320 yard-long curtain wall surrounding it conceals another one within, making a double barrier to add to the considerable inconvenience caused by a wide moat. During July and August, and on bank holidays outside those months, visitors can get an invaders' eye view of Caerphilly's defences, when regular boat tours travel the waters of the moat.

Inside, Caerphilly Castle's Great Hall is still one of its most striking features. An exhibition of the castles of Wales is housed in the north-west tower, while one in the outer east gate takes the town of Caerphilly as its subject.

Caerphilly Castle is open to the public all year, though times vary according to the season.

OAKWOOD ADVENTURE AND LEISURE PARK
Near Narberth, Pembrokeshire

Half an hour's drive from Carmarthen, an hour from Swansea and 90 minutes away from Cardiff, Oakwood Park is set in 80 acres of beautiful countryside. From the large (free) car park, a miniature train carries visitors to Oakwood Station, the starting point for a variety of attractions.

As well as thrilling rides, there are assault courses and the Skyleap, an exhilarating free-fall slide. Go-karting facilities are tailored to the needs of both young children and older riders. Rowing boats and kayaks for use on the boating lake can be hired.

The biggest covered play area in South Wales, containing a range of activities suitable for young children, offers all-weather entertainment. Those in search of peace and quiet can find it when they explore some of the Park's nature trails, which include a special Young Explorer's Trail through the different habitats of the Park.

Oakwood is open daily from Good Friday until the end of September. Though dogs are not allowed in the Park, free kennels mean that they can be accommodated while their owners spend time there. Refreshment facilities for humans include a licensed restaurant serving home cooked meals, fast food outlets, and picnic areas.

BIG PIT Blaenafon, near Abergavenny, Gwent

Big Pit stopped operating as a working colliery in 1980, exactly 100 years after it first started producing coal. The pit is now a museum where visitors can find out how miners have lived and worked over the last 200 years.

Exhibitions illustrate the history of the coal industry in south Wales, and show how

Toboggans and go-karts – just two of the attractions at Oakwood Park.

mining communities lived. The miners' canteen now offers a range of refreshments.

The highlight of a visit to Big Pit, however, is surely the chance to explore the colliery's underground workings with ex-miners as guides. Kitted out in safety-helmets, cap lamps and self-rescuers just like working miners, visitors enter the pit cage for the 294-foot journey down to the bottom of the shaft. The walk through the workings, some of which pre-date Big Pit, takes about an hour and introduces many relics of mining history. The coal-faces, haulage engines and stables where pit ponies used to be kept are all here.

Big Pit is open every day between March and December and practical shoes and warm clothes are essential. However, small children cannot be taken underground.

DAN-YR-OGOF SHOWCAVES
Abercraf, Powys

Open seven days a week from Easter until the end of October, the Dan-yr-Ogof Showcave Complex is the largest of its kind in Europe.

Buy perfume made by monks, and visit the Shrine to Our Lady, at Caldy Island.

Created underneath the southern fringes of Brecon Beacons National Park by the action of acidic water on limestone, this network of caves and caverns contains some of the best rock, stalactite and stalagmite formations on public view anywhere. Firm, dry walkways lead to the Dan-yr-Ogof Showcave (Britain's longest showcave), Cathedral Showcave (the largest single chamber in any British showcave) and the Bone Cave, where Bronze Age man made his home 3000 years ago. All are floodlit.

Also at Dan-yr-Ogof is the award-winning Dinosaur Park, complete with reconstructions of huge prehistoric monsters, a museum and audiovisual theatre, a craft shop and Tourist Information Centre, and restaurant and picnic facilities. An unusual bonus is an artificial ski slope, where instruction is available.

CALDY ISLAND Dyfed

Men have lived on Caldy Island, now twenty minutes by boat out of Tenby Harbour, since prehistoric times. Cistercian monks now farm the 1½-mile-long island, though the Benedictines preceded them; the island's church and part of its monastery date from medieval times.

Caldy's most famous export is its perfume, made by the monks who live on the island, from the flowers and herbs that grow there. They also produce clotted cream, yoghurts and cakes.

Caldy is also home to colonies of seals and sea birds, best seen from one of the boats which frequently cruise around the island.

TREDEGAR HOUSE AND COUNTRY PARK Newport, Gwent

Tredegar House gives many clues to the wealth, power and influence of the family who lived there, from Llewellyn ap Morgan

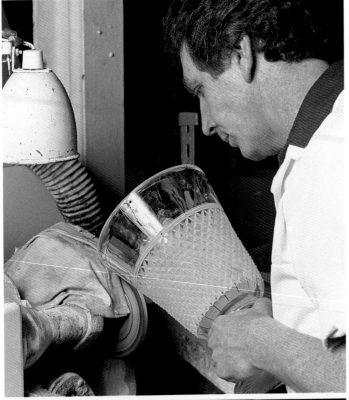

in 1402 to the last Lord of Tredegar who died in 1962. Only one wing of the original medieval manor house remains: Tredegar owes most of its present-day character to extensive 17th-century rebuilding, and to the addition, 200 years later, of a new servants' wing and service corridors to cope with the growing domestic needs of the house's occupants.

Tours of the house, for which a charge is made, take place on specified days between Easter and the end of October. They take in both 'upstairs' and 'downstairs' so that visitors can get the complete picture of how a country house and its estate operated in years gone by.

The 1000 acres of land surrounding the house provided for all the daily needs of its residents and staff. Many of the estate buildings have been restored and put to new uses: the Brewhouse, appropriately enough, contains a range of refreshment facilities, and the former implement sheds of the home farm now house craft workshops.

Open all year, the 90-acre Country Park offers beautiful walks and nature trails, fishing in the coarse season and, in the summer season only, children's donkey rides and boating. Limited space in the Park is available for caravanners and campers, but advance booking is essential.

STUART CRYSTAL FACTORY
Bargoed, Mid Glamorgan

Free guided tours of the Stuart Crystal Factory at Bargoed introduce visitors to the blowing and decorating of beautiful crystal glass.

Tours take place Monday–Friday all year round, except for factory holidays (Easter Monday and Tuesday, spring bank holiday week, the last week in July, the first week in August, and around Christmas and New

At Stuart Crystal visitors have the opportunity to watch craftsmen gilding and engraving hand made crystal.

Year), and the first of the day sets off at 10am. Advance booking is essential for groups of eight people or more, and potential visitors should note that, for safety reasons, the tour is unsuitable for children under the age of four years.

CARDIFF South Glamorgan

Cardiff has only been the Welsh capital since 1955, but the city's origins go back almost 2000 years. Traces of a Roman fort, thought to have been built by a commander called Dydd – hence the settlement's Welsh name,

Cardiff Castle is part Roman fort, part medieval stronghold, and part 19th-century mansion.

The Banqueting Hall in Bute Tower (above, left), the kitchen (above), china in the National Museum of Wales (below, right) and Cardiff Castle (below) are just a few of the attractions in Cardiff.

'Caerdydd' (seat of Dydd) – are still visible in Cardiff Castle's outer walls, though later occupants adapted it to suit their own needs. Extensively restored by the Marquess of Bute in the 19th century, and with new Victorian-style buildings added at that time, Cardiff Castle is now one of the city's major attractions. Medieval banquets are held here, and it houses two regimental museums.

Ornamental panels within the castle depict its turbulent history, but the scope widens to include the whole of Wales in the National Museum, Cathays Park. Welsh plants and animals, and the geological forces that shaped the landscape, are illustrated, and there are fine collections representing the work and art of the people. A superb array of modern paintings and

Castell Coch is a Victorian whimsy built by an eccentric genius for the Marquess of Bute.

A bedroom in the fairy tale Castell Coch.

sculpture from all over Europe is on display. Other aspects of Welsh history and culture are covered by the Welsh Folk Museum, and the Welsh Industrial and Maritime Museum in the city's docklands.

Cathays Park is also a showcase for the best of 20th-century municipal architecture: many impressive public buildings are here in what has been called one of the finest civic centres in Europe.

On the outskirts of the city, Llandaff Cathedral – restored since it was devastated by World War Two bombing – now includes Epstein's awesome sculpture, *Christ in Majesty.*

In common with other major European cities, Cardiff is an important arts and enter-tainment centre. Live theatre, music and dance events are held at The New Theatre and St David's Hall, the latter the national concert and conference hall of Wales. The Sherman Theatre is home of Cardiff's Repertory Theatre, while around 150 arts and entertainment events of all kinds are mounted every month at the Chapter Arts centre. The Welsh National Opera and Welsh Jazz Society are based in Cardiff, and the annual Festival of Cardiff brings a variety of artistes to the city every year in late July and early August.

Winter and summer, there are plenty of sporting and recreational facilities for both spectators and participants. A number of leisure centres in and around the city are open to the public, and other venues offer the chance to enjoy cricket, baseball, golf, tennis, bowls and sailing. Cardiff Arms Park is the home of Welsh rugby union, and of the National Sports Centre. An international standard athletics track, Olympic sized swimming pool and the Welsh National Ice Rink bring competitors from all over the world to Wales.

Most of Cardiff's compact central shopping area, a short walk from the city's railway and bus stations, is traffic free. Here are a range of department stores and specialist shops, and there are markets both under cover and out of doors.

FOR FURTHER INFORMATION CONTACT:

Tourist Information Centre
8–14 Bridge Street
CARDIFF
South Glamorgan CF5 2EJ
Telephone: (0222) 227281

Wales Tourist Board
Brunel House
2 Fitzalan Road
CARDIFF CF2 1UY
Telephone: (0222) 499909

NORTH WEST

Blackpool Tower seen from the beach.

The beautiful corner of England that embraces Lancashire and Cheshire is where the Romans settled and the Industrial Revolution began, and it is a veritable land of British heritage.

Cheshire is one of England's lesser known counties, but is also one of its most beautiful. The county has a central fertile plain, and is dotted with meres and rivers sheltered by woodlands. Many of the churches are made from red sandstone, while black and white houses are also characteristic of this part of England.

Part of the county sits on a rock-salt bed and salt has been mined in Northwich since Roman times. Silk was also once manufactured in the county at Macclesfield but many of the old mills have either been demolished or are converted for other uses. The chief administrative centre of Cheshire is Chester which was an important military centre during Roman occupation. Evidence of this occupation is the Roman amphitheatre – one of the largest to be excavated in Britain.

The neighbouring county of Merseyside is mostly renowned for its more recent history as the birthplace of the Beatles pop group and the 1960s mersey-beat sound. It is also famous for its two legendary football clubs – Everton and Liverpool. Situated on the north bank of the River Mersey, Liverpool has been an important port since the mid-19th century. The docks now cover seven miles and are among the finest in the world. Traditionally the area is a glass-making and soap-manufacturing district. St Helens is the home of Pilkingtons, the glass manufacturers, and nearby Port Sunlight – a village named after Sunlight Soap – helped build the fortune of William Lever.

Further north, Lancashire was once a mining area, and in the 19th century was the largest cotton manufacturer in the world. Today it is an area of dairy farming, market gardening and modern industries including textiles, mining and engineering. Blackpool, Morecambe and Southport form the heart of the tourist industry. These have sandy beaches and traditional attractions. Morecambe is also a haven for naturalists who can walk across the bay at low tide.

Gourmets to the region will find a variety of dairy produce, including Cheshire and Lancashire cheese. There is also an abundance of sea food, and being a cosmopolitan district, a variety of take-away food from across the world.

LANCASTER

LANCASHIRE

BLACKPOOL

BURNLEY

PRESTON

BLACKBURN

BOLTON

OLDHAM

GREATER MANCHESTER

MERSEYSIDE

ST. HELENS

MANCHESTER

WALLASEY

LIVERPOOL

STOCKPORT

MACCLESFIELD

CHESHIRE

CHESTER

CREWE

NORTH WEST

1	Jodrell Bank
2	Ellesmere Boat Museum
3	Museum of Science & Industry
4	Hall-I'-Th'-Wood
5	Norton Priory
6	Tatton Park
7	Leighton Hall
8	Steamtown
9	Wigan Pier
10	Blackpool Pleasure Beach
11	Camelot Theme Park
12	Knowsley Safari Park
13	Stapeley Water Gardens
14	Port Sunlight Village
15	Speedwell Cavern
16	Last Drop Village

SPEEDWELL CAVERN
Near Castleton, Derbyshire

Literally in the heart of Derbyshire's glorious Peak District, the underground Speedwell Cavern was once part of an 18th-century lead mine. Finds were small and mining was discontinued after about twenty years, but not before part of the underground workings was flooded – possibly, it is thought, to make a canal along which the lead ore could be transported.

Present-day visitors to Speedwell Cavern travel along the half-mile illuminated canal in boats propelled by experienced guides. At the end of the canal, over 800 feet below ground, the narrow tunnel suddenly and dramatically opens out at the awe-inspiring Bottomless Pit. Its depths guarded for safety by strong iron railings, the Pit once swallowed up 40,000 tons of rubble without any change in its water level. Water pours down here and disappears for 22 hours before resurfacing at a natural spring in Castleton, only half a mile away.

Boats leave on their tour every fifteen minutes, and the Cavern is open daily thoughout the year.

THE BOAT MUSEUM
Ellesmere Port, Cheshire

When the Industrial Revolution hit northern England and transformed it into one of the primary manufacturing areas in the country, it did so with the help of an extensive canal network that carried raw materials to the factories and finished products from them. Two of the most important waterways – the Shropshire Union and the Manchester Ship canals – meet at Ellesmere Port amid a remarkable group of buildings that date from the era's heyday, and which now form part of the port's Boat Museum.

Based around a dock complex which includes the locks that drop the waterways between old offices and warehouses, the museum houses the world's largest collection of inland waterways craft. Tugs, narrowboats, wide boats, ice-breakers and coastal craft from rivers and canals all over Britain have been restored at the museum: as well as being able to see some of the traditional boat-building techniques used, visitors can go on board many of the craft and experience how their crews lived and worked.

Visitors travel along the illuminated canal at Speedwell Cavern, an 18th-century lead mine.

Indoor exhibitions in dockside buildings tell the story of the canals and the boats that used them. Restored steam engines, which once powered the 40 cranes and nineteen capstans in use around the dock, are on show in The Pump House. Passing boats still use the two flights of locks which drop the Shropshire Union Canal to the lower basin and its junction with the Manchester Ship Canal. Victorian dock-workers' cottages have been refurbished to show how their occupants lived from the late 19th century until the 1950s, and a resident blacksmith still works in the forge where the horses which once pulled the canal boats were shod.

Open all year (but closed on winter Fridays), though times vary according to the season, the Boat Museum also offers boat trips, shopping and catering facilities.

LIVERPOOL Merseyside

Although Liverpool was first established as a port in the 13th century, its real rise to prominence began 500 years later. Early exports included slaves and sugar to the West Indies but, as the Industrial Revolution gathered momentum in the second half of the 18th century, the scope widened to include many of the products of England's new manufacturing economy.

At one time, the banks of the River Mersey on which the city stands boasted 35 miles of quayside: in the early 19th century, Liverpool's seven miles of docks handled almost half of Britain's exports. In the 100 years from 1830, nine million passengers passed through Liverpool on their way to the New World. Evidence of the waterfront's commercial importance remains in the shape of impressive constructions like the Port of Liverpool Building (1907), the Liver Building (1910) and the Cunard Building (1917).

Liverpool's prosperity may have been built on industry and commerce, but its

The Boat Museum, Ellesmere Port (opposite page); the Albert Dock Maritime Museum (right).

inhabitants also established it as an important cultural centre. St George's Hall, the Picton Library, Liverpool Museum and the Walker Art Gallery cluster in neo-classical splendour in William Brown Street, and contain some fine archaeological, artistic and literary collections.

The 'live' arts flourish: city centre theatres include the Liverpool Empire, Playhouse, Everyman, Neptune and Unity, and programmes range from the avant-garde to the traditional. The city that produced The Beatles is also home to the world famous Royal Liverpool Philharmonic Orchestra, which performs around 75 public concerts a year in The Philharmonic Hall. Lunchtime recitals at the city's Anglican and Roman Catholic cathedrals are an extra reason to visit two fine 20th-century buildings: both majestic and awe-inspiring, they are completely different in character and style.

Changing economic circumstances have meant that Liverpool can no longer rely only on its seaport and manufacturing facilities for prosperity. Tourism has emerged as a major new industry, and much has been done to revitalise many of the waterfront areas which fell into decline when they were no longer needed for their original purpose.

One of the most spectacular developments has been at Albert Dock, the UK's largest group of Grade 1 listed buildings. This complex of restored Victorian warehouses is now home to the Merseyside Maritime Museum (open daily), a unique blend of original buildings, floating exhibits, craft demonstrations, working displays and special events telling the story of the city's development into Britain's second-largest port. The Tate Gallery Liverpool is here, too, complementing the city's other fine art galleries. Now one of the top visitor attractions in England, Albert Dock also houses a variety of shops, restaurants and bars – all within surroundings designed to re-create the relaxed elegance of Victorian times.

Sporting facilities are excellent, both for participants and spectators. The oldest Chinatown in Europe offers some of the finest Oriental cuisine in the country. Transport links within the city and to outlying areas are based on ferries, road and rail, bringing the Lancashire coastal resorts, North Wales, the Lake District and Chester within easy reach.

The Merseyside Maritime Museum relates the story of Liverpool's development into Britain's second largest port.

TATTON PARK Knutsford, Cheshire

A thousand-acre estate complete with a mile-long lake, deer park and formal gardens – not to mention one of the best-preserved Georgian mansions in the country containing important furniture, Italian works of art and books – all combine to make Tatton Park one of Britain's most popular stately homes.

Designed by Samuel Wyatt for the Egertons at the beginning of the 19th century, and incorporating some of the features of an earlier building, the present house stands on an estate held by the family since Elizabethan days. Its picture collection includes works by Canaletto and Van Dyck; the furniture is original and from some of Europe's finest designers; the library's collections go back to the 16th century.

Visitors to the house can experience both the grandeur of the rooms inhabited by those who lived 'upstairs', and the more functional surroundings of the 'downstairs' staff whose job it was to make sure that their

Japanese garden and Shinto Temple (right and below) at Tatton Park.

employers did not have to worry about putting food on the table and keeping the place clean.

Subsequent generations of Egertons built on their forebears' collections rather than replacing them: the last lord, who left Tatton to the National Trust in 1958, was a pioneer aviator and motor traveller (his 1900 Benz is on view) – and a passionate big-game hunter. He built Tenants' Hall to house his macabre trophies.

Wyatt's Orangery, complete with orange trees and other exotic plants, still stands but it was Humphry Repton who was responsible for first landscaping the 54 acres of formal gardens surrounding the house. He also had some influence on the appearance of the estate as a whole, which now offers excellent facilities for visitors – including fishing, riding, nature trails, a deer park and Home Farm.

CAMELOT THEME PARK
Near Chorley, Lancashire

As its name suggests, the attractions at Camelot Theme Park are all based around Arthurian legend. Play facilities, rides and special medieval-style events combine to offer families a truly magical day out. A single entrance fee covers admission to all the entertainment.

Small children have their own scaled-down rides and indoor play areas, and they are welcome to help feed the animals at the Petting Zoo. Rides like the Tower of Terror, which rises 100 feet before plunging into the abyss, test the bravery of older members of the family, as does the journey into the lair of the foul-hearted Beast. The Falcon's Flight Balloon Ride whirls its passengers high in the air, while the Camelot Cascade is a spectacular water-chute.

Trumpets and thundering hooves herald the start of the Royal Jousting Tournament, where the crowds are encouraged to cheer their champions to victory. Duels are fought, with the combatants using weapons ranging from mighty broadswords to spiked maces. Jesters, minstrels, strolling players and street artists provide their own special brand of entertainment.

On fine days, the outdoor Splashpool – complete with Serpent water-slide – helps young visitors cool off after all the excitement.

A number of restaurants cater for varying tastes and budgets; shops, each based on its own theme, sell gifts and souvenirs.

JODRELL BANK SCIENCE CENTRE AND GRANADA ARBORETUM
Near Macclesfield, Cheshire

Thirty years after one of the world's largest steerable radio telescopes first went into service, its cathedral-sized saucer still dominates the Cheshire Plain and marks the site of Jodrell Bank. Its job is to 'see' into space by picking up the radio signals sent out by stars, planets and other extra-terrestrial bodies, and it is the subject of only one of the exhibitions open to the public at Jodrell Bank Science Centre.

All kinds of scientific and technological marvels are on view here, and the emphasis is on interactive displays that allow visitors actually to experience some of the phenomena the exhibits describe. Infinity, gravity and spinning forces are just a few of the experiences that can be explored, and there is a chance to steer a seven-metre model telescope and track the stars.

Regular tours of the universe start at the Planetarium, where the computer-controlled journey changes with the seasons. Each 'tour' lasts about 25 minutes and, because they take place in almost complete darkness, they are not suitable for children under five years of age.

Thanks to technological wizardry, Sir Isaac Newton – or, at least, his talking head – is there to explain his theories on gravity and planetary motion. Coming right up to

The cathedral-sized saucer at Jodrell Bank.

date, there is an introduction to satellite television and holograms and, because Jodrell Bank is still a working research station, information about the Centre's current and future projects.

Surrounding the Science Centre is the 40-acre Arboretum, with impressive collections of trees and shrubs as well as heather and rose gardens. Marked trails introduce walks lasting between 30 minutes and 1½ hours, and there are picnic and play areas.

Jodrell Bank is open daily from Easter to the end of October, and in the afternoons of winter weekends and Christmas holidays.

Steamtown Carnforth, Lancashire

Steam locomotives ranging from giant passenger engines, through no-nonsense freight-haulers to tiny tank engines are on display at Steamtown, the largest operating mainline steam depot in England.

Carnforth engine shed was last used by British Rail in 1968, and was one of their last steam depots. When BR's connection with it ended, Steamtown was born, continuing the tradition that had linked Carnforth with steam-powered travel since the earliest railway days.

As well as over 30 locomotives, Steamtown houses restored passenger coaches and freight wagons. Britain's last working coaling tower is here, as is one of the signal boxes that once helped ensure the safe passage of trains travelling the famous Settle-to-Carlisle route, and which can still be seen in operation.

A fifteen-inch gauge miniature railway — complete with scaled-down stations, signals and covered coaches — has its own mile-long track, and an even smaller model

An early Sunlight soap poster.

railway layout is on display in a carriage.

Though Steamtown is open all year, except around Christmas, its main programme of activity days is concentrated in the months between Easter and October. Details of what happens when are published in a leaflet available from Steamtown.

Port Sunlight Wirral, Merseyside

One of the north west's great industrialists, William Hesketh Lever (later the first Viscount Leverhulme), founded the garden village of Port Sunlight in 1888 to house the workers who staffed his soap factory. Around 30 architects were employed to create his vision of 'a new Arcadia', where varied architecture and open spaces contrasted dramatically with the cheap, functional workers' housing provided elsewhere in the north west by factory and mill-owners.

Port Sunlight is now a conservation area, still within its original boundaries. A Heritage Centre explores the history of the village and the people who have lived there, and the Village Trail takes in all the village's attractions. These include the Lady Lever Art Gallery and Museum which holds Lord Leverhulme's own collection of fine paintings, sculpture, furniture, tapestries, Wedgwood pottery and Chinese porcelain.

Blackpool Lancashire

When the railway arrived in Blackpool in the mid-19th century to link the coast with the industrial towns of Lancashire and Yorkshire, people first discovered the chance to get away from their smoke-filled

The famous Blackpool Illuminations light up in September and October.

environments and find fresh air and relaxation within easy reach. Since then, those in search of a seaside holiday have gone to Blackpool to find it. Even while the guaranteed sunshine of the Mediterranean has lured some away, families continue to brave Blackpool's unpredictable climate and enjoy the traditional pleasures of one of Britain's premier coastal resorts.

Blackpool's Pleasure Beach provides 40 acres of entertainment. Palm Court (below, right) at Stapeley Water Gardens.

Blackpool's most famous landmark is its Tower. Built in the 1890s in imitation of the Eiffel Tower in Paris, it is just over half the height of the original. Except in windy conditions, its lift carries passengers 518 feet up for a breath-taking view from the top. A fine aquarium, a zoo, a circus and a ballroom are all housed in the Tower.

Blackpool's beach stretches for six miles, and there are three piers offering all sorts of holiday amusements. The last commercial tramway in England still travels the full seven-mile length of the Promenade, at the heart of which is the Golden Mile with its amusement arcades, hot-dog stalls and candy-floss stands. At the southern end of the Golden Mile, the Pleasure Beach covers 40 acres with roller coasters, big wheels and other thrilling rides − more, so it claims, than any other amusement park in the world. New attractions and special events are added every year: part of Blackpool's policy of continuous development to keep ahead of the opposition.

The town's holiday season stretches into the autumn. In September and October, the famous Blackpool Illuminations light up the Tower, Promenade and the Pleasure Beach, and even the decorated trams take on fantastic illuminated shapes.

Those needing to escape from the frenetic activity that characterises Britain's largest holiday resort can find tranquillity in Stanley Gardens. Not far from the Golden Mile, the site offers Italian-style gardens, an enormous boating lake, and facilities for bowls, tennis and golf. Around 30,000 blooms make for a fabulous summer-time display in the rose gardens here, and the conservatories house around 700 species of chrysanthemums.

STAPELEY WATER GARDENS
Near Nantwich, Cheshire

Europe's largest water-garden centre covers 35 acres. On display − and on sale − are a variety of water-based features for gardens of all shapes and sizes. A team of experts is on hand to advise visitors on the kind of pool, fountain or waterfall that would best enhance their garden.

Cold water and tropical fish are on sale, too, in what is said to be one of the most modern aquarist centres in the UK. Again, knowledgeable advice is on hand.

Water-garden plants − for margins and for planting under water − are on show; there are over 50 varieties of water-lily alone.

Admission to the garden centre is free, as is car-parking, but there is a charge to visit

The Palms, a giant heated glasshouse that covers an acre of land. Piranhas lurk under the massive leaves of Amazonian water-lilies; the cries of tropical birds mingle with the sound of cascading water, and the whole environment is designed to create an impression of lush rain-forest vegetation with its associated wildlife.

On a less exotic note, land-based hardy plants and house-plants are also on sale. Expert staff can advise on plant selection, as well as on the best tools and other products for particular garden tasks.

MUSEUM OF SCIENCE AND INDUSTRY
Castlefield, Manchester

Located in historic buildings in central Manchester, the Museum of Science and Industry brings the city's past vividly to life. Hundreds of exhibits, many in full working order, tell the story of people and machines which helped turn Manchester into one of the developed world's most important cities, and which laid the foundations of modern industry.

The world's largest collection of stationary steam engines is on display in the Power Hall, where railway locomotives are also on view. Vintage cars and motor-cycles help illustrate the development of the internal combustion engine.

The four-floor National Electricity Gallery shows how the industry developed until it revolutionised people's everyday lives, while the Air and Space Gallery brings the power story right up to date with some of the craft that have made aviation history.

A reconstructed Victorian sewer is the centrepiece of the 'Underground Manchester' exhibition, which complements another on the historical and social development of the area.

Part of the Castlefield Urban Heritage Park, the first of its kind in England, the Museum of Science and Industry is Europe's largest industrial museum. Also part of the Park are G-Mex, an international exhibition centre; Castlefield Gallery, housing displays of contemporary arts; and an imaginative reconstruction of a Roman fort.

Manchester's Museum of Science and Industry offers visitors a chance to experience the city's past.

HALL-I'-TH'-WOOD MUSEUM
Bolton, Greater Manchester

Built in the 15th century and added to by those who owned it over the next 200 years, Hall-i'-th'-Wood is a typical Lancashire merchant's house of its period and open to the public between April and September.

The beautiful oak panelling and impressive plaster ceilings in some of the rooms were installed by Alexander Norris, who inherited the house in 1639. The property has remained largely unaltered since then, though Lord Leverhulme bought and restored it before handing it over to Bolton Corporation in 1902.

Hall-i'-th'-Wood was once the home of Samuel Crompton, who invented the spinning mule in 1779, and his life is illustrated in displays which include the workroom in which the mule was invented. The kitchen has been restored to show how it might have looked in Crompton's time, and is complete with original pieces of equipment. Intricately crafted stairways lead to rooms which house some fine furniture, and where aspects of Bolton's history are explored.

The old part of Hall-i'-th'-Wood dates from the 15th century and its newest wing was added in 1648.

KNOWSLEY SAFARI PARK
Prescot, Merseyside

Five miles of roads wind through parkland in the grounds of the Earl of Derby's Knowsley Park estate. A journey along them is more like a trek through the African bush than anything else: herds of eland, buffalo, bison and zebra graze alongside the road. Lions, tigers and African elephants also populate the game reserve, and inquisitive monkeys find visitors just as interesting as the visitors find them.

By way of contrast, Pets Corner offers young children the chance to get close to the tame domestic animals, and an amusement park also caters for their special needs.

For safety reasons, soft-topped cars are restricted to parts of the park where animals cannot get too close; drivers of such vehicles are welcome to travel on the Park's Safari Bus when it is available.

Knowsley Safari Park is open daily from 1st March until 31st October, 10am-4pm.

Lechwe deer (above) and rhinoceroses (below) at Knowsley Safari Park.

The largest collection of trained birds of prey in the north of England is found at Leighton Hall.

The Last Drop Village's name was the outcome of a discussion between the owner and a friend over who should drink the 'last drop' of wine during a meal.

LEIGHTON HALL Carnforth, Lancashire

Leighton Hall has been home of the famous furniture-making Gillow family for over 400 years, and is still a private house set in rolling parkland against a backdrop of the Lakeland Fells.

Guided tours of the Hall last about 45 minutes. There are neither ropes nor barriers, and the emphasis is on welcoming visitors to a real family home where all the rooms are actually lived in. Some fine examples of early Gillow furniture are on display; there are some notable paintings, and interesting collections of English and French clocks and other *objets d'art.*

Attractive gardens, including a walled garden and open maze, are close to the Hall, while woodland walks take visitors further afield. The largest collection of trained birds of prey in the north of England is here, too, and there are regular flying displays. Many of the native birds in the collection were rescued, injured, from the wild.

Leighton Hall is open to the public from May to September (afternoons only; closed Saturdays and Mondays). Special events are held throughout the year (details from the Hall). Parties of adults and schoolchildren are welcome, and arrangements can be made in advance for them to visit outside normal opening hours.

THE LAST DROP VILLAGE
Bromley Cross, Lancashire

In 1964, Orrellford was a collection of derelict 18th-century farm buildings. It has now been transformed into an imaginatively-designed traditional style village complete with hotel, pub and health club facilities.

Two restaurants cater for both formal and informal dining needs, while The Drop Inn re-creates a traditional local pub complete with regular honky-tonk piano evenings.

Centrepiece of the village is an 83-bedroom luxury hotel. Its extensive leisure facilities include a heated indoor swimming pool, wavepool, whirlpool bath, sauna, steam room, sun beds, gymnasium and squash court.

WIGAN PIER HERITAGE CENTRE
Wigan, Lancashire

Wigan was in existence long before it became one of northern England's great 19th-century industrial centres. The Romans had a fort there, coal was mined in the area, and by 1400 Wigan was a thriving weaving and market town.

The Industrial Revolution arrived in Wigan with the Leeds and Liverpool Canal in 1779, which dramatically improved communications — especially freight transport — between the old Lancashire towns. Iron-working, engineering and textile businesses flourished. Nowadays much of the heavy industry has gone, and the last big colliery closed in 1967.

Wigan Pier Heritage Centre recaptures the life of the town as it was in the early years of the 20th century. It is a living museum. Members of the Centre's own theatre company re-create some of the people who lived and worked in the town almost 100 years ago so that visitors can talk to them about what was going on at the time.

Shop-keepers, tinsmiths, clog-makers, publicans and miners are at work, and daily demonstrations of working machinery recall the days when Wigan's textile industry thrived. In nearby Trencherfield Mill is the 2500 horsepower, horizontal, four-cylinder condensing engine that turns a 70-ton fly-wheel. The largest working mill steam engine in the world is set in motion daily.

NORTON PRIORY MUSEUM AND GARDENS *Runcorn, Cheshire*

The ruins and undercroft of Norton Priory — the largest monastic archaeological excavations in Britain — are to be found within a sixteen-acre woodland garden which also houses reminders of the site's later occupants.

Life in 12th-century Cheshire, as it would have been when Norton Priory was originally built for Augustinian monks, is re-created in exhibitions and displays mounted in the prize-winning museum on the site. Age-old crafts and artforms such as tile-making, sculpture and carving are revived and celebrated in regular workshops, exhibitions and demonstrations; the year-round programme of events also includes guided tours.

The Georgian manor house constructed on the site for the Brooke family was demolished in 1928, but the walled garden built by Sir Richard Brooke in the 18th century has now been restored. Originally part of an extension scheme that included plans for stables and an ice-house, the garden — managed by the head gardener and his eight staff — would have provided fruit and vegetables for the manor house. No longer needed once the family moved away, it fell into neglect until the early 1980s.

Now brought back to life under the auspices of the Runcorn Development Corporation to reflect both Georgian and modern designs and uses, the Walled Garden is a treat for gardeners and casual strollers alike. Those who founded it would probably recognise some of its features — a rose walk, herb garden, fruit arch and vegetable plots — though some of the plants it now contains would have been less familiar.

Norton Priory is open throughout the year, though times vary according to the season.

Norton Priory includes the largest monastic archaeological excavations in Britain.

CHESTER Cheshire

One of the most important Roman military bases in England, Chester was already ancient when William the Conqueror created its earldom in 1070. Well-preserved medieval walls, complete with Roman and Saxon fragments, enclose the old city: within them is the maze of narrow streets that characterise Chester.

The Eastgate, topped by an ornate clock erected to celebrate Queen Victoria's Jubilee, is still – as it was in medieval times – the main entrance to Chester, and there are superb views from the top of it. A walkway all round the top of the walls means that visitors can introduce themselves easily to the town, as well as the surrounding countryside.

Black and white 'magpie' buildings are a typical feature of Chester's streets.

It was the Victorians who added more dazzling black and white 'magpie' buildings to those already present in the town centre, and who restored the Rows. These are an architectural feature unique among English towns – raised covered galleries with shops at first-floor level, and another tier of shops at street level underneath.

Chester's cathedral, St Werburgh's, has its origin in an 11th-century Benedictine Abbey and is approached via the massive 14th-century Abbey Gateway. Its architecture reflects all the variations in Gothic style common between the 13th and 16th centuries, and there are regular audiovisual displays covering the cathedral's history.

One of Chester's medieval parish churches, St Michael's, is now the home of the Chester Heritage Centre. Exhibitions and

CHESTER

Chester's well-preserved medieval walls enclose the old city which is a maze of narrow streets. Part of the city wall and King Charles Tower (top, left); lovely walkways beneath half-timbered buildings (above, right); Queen's Park Bridge and River Dee (below).

Chester owes much to the Victorians architecturally, for they so admired the magpie buildings that they built even more of them.

displays illustrate the town's history, architecture and award-winning conservation programmes. Opening times vary according to the time of year. Other aspects of the town's history are on view at the Chester Visitor Centre, the Grosvenor Museum, and Chester Military Museum in Chester Castle.

Britain's largest zoo outside London is two miles out of town, set in 100 acres of magnificent landscaped gardens. Many rare and endangered species breed here in spacious enclosures; there are few cages, as moats are used instead to confine the animals. Chester Zoo is open every day.

Chester City Council's Tourism Promotion Unit produces a regular *What's on in Chester* brochure which features all sorts of events taking place in and around the city. Drama, music (classical, jazz, folk, blues, pop), sport, and lectures on interests ranging from history to horticulture, archaeology to embroidery, are all covered.

FOR FURTHER INFORMATION CONTACT:

Tourist Information Centre
29 Lime Street
LIVERPOOL
Merseyside L1 1JG
Telephone: (051) 709 3631

Tourist Information Centre
Town Hall
Northgate Street
CHESTER
Cheshire CH1 2NF
Telephone: (0244) 324324

North West Tourist Board
The Last Drop Village
Bromley Cross
BOLTON
Lancashire BL7 9PZ
Telephone: (0204) 591511

NORTH YORKSHIRE AND HUMBERSIDE

Staithes, North Yorkshire.

North Yorkshire and Humberside are counties of immense natural beauty that are as contrasting as they are beautiful. The coastline is officially designated a 'Heritage Coast' and there are high cliffs, broad bays, expansive beaches and smugglers' coves. Inland, the rugged beauty of the North Yorkshire Moors stretches from above the plain of York to the sea and contrasts with the bustling industrial towns of Leeds and Bradford.

The coastline has a long maritime tradition and many of the small villages have been dominated by the fishing industry for centuries. The villages are lined with terraces and frequented by anglers and yachtsman who are annually drawn to the numerous yachting and angling events at Scarborough, Whitby and Filey.

The mud flats at the tip of Spurn Head support a wide variety of wildlife indigenous only to salt flats, and Humberside has three RSPB reserves. The North Yorkshire Moors host an abundance of wildlife among the wild heather of late summer, and the golden bracken of autumn.

During its long history the coastline has been the site of numerous invasions. The country has been home to invading Romans, Saxons, Danes, and Normans who have left behind a legacy of historic buildings, many of which still stand today. The area incorporates many religious sites including the most impressive monastic site in Britain at Whitby, and the recently restored York Minster – Britain's largest Gothic Church.

As a mining and industrial centre the prosperity of the area underwent a revival during the 18th and 19th centuries. Evidence of this is revealed in the many large country houses scattered around the countryside, such as Castle Howard, still home to the legendary Howard family.

The 18th century was also the era of northern craftsmen with men like Adams, famous for the fine plaster ceilings, and Thomas Chippendale, a legend in the world of furniture making.

As an area of agricultural land, Yorkshire and Humberside has a wealth of food and drink to offer the intrepid traveller. Beer is a regional favourite, and meat is also high on the local menu with locally cooked hams, spare ribs, pork pies, faggots and black pudding available in most butchers shops.

As a fishing area for many years the coastline was dotted with smoking houses and today a handful remain which still sell traditional fare including smoked kippers and salmon.

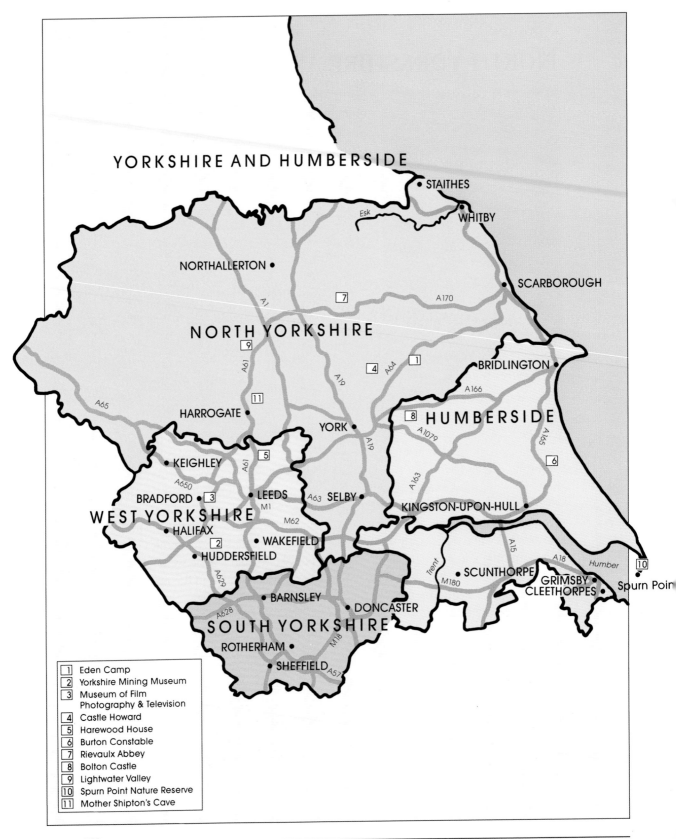

YORKSHIRE AND HUMBERSIDE

STAITHES

WHITBY

Esk

NORTHALLERTON

SCARBOROUGH

7

NORTH YORKSHIRE

A1

A170

9

A61

4 A64   1

BRIDLINGTON

11

A166

HARROGATE

8 HUMBERSIDE

A61

A19

YORK

A1079

A19

A65

A163

A165

6

5

KEIGHLEY

A61

A650

BRADFORD   3   LEEDS

A63   SELBY

KINGSTON-UPON-HULL

M1

WEST YORKSHIRE

HALIFAX

M62

2   WAKEFIELD

HUDDERSFIELD

A15

Humber

10

A629

Trent

SCUNTHORPE

A18

Spurn Point

BARNSLEY

M180

GRIMSBY

DONCASTER

CLEETHORPES

A628

SOUTH YORKSHIRE

M18

ROTHERHAM

SHEFFIELD   A57

1	Eden Camp
2	Yorkshire Mining Museum
3	Museum of Film Photography & Television
4	Castle Howard
5	Harewood House
6	Burton Constable
7	Rievaulx Abbey
8	Bolton Castle
9	Lightwater Valley
10	Spurn Point Nature Reserve
11	Mother Shipton's Cave

BURTON CONSTABLE HALL
Sproatley, near Hull

Set in parkland and lakes once landscaped by Capability Brown, Burton Constable Hall at Sproatley is the home of Mr John Chichester Constable whose title is the 'Lord Paramount of the Seigniory of Holderness'. This title was inherited from a Norman ancestor who came over with William the Conqueror.

Built in 1570 the house is a magnificent Elizabethan mansion with 18th-century additions by architects Adam, Lightoller, Carr and Wyatt. The Great Hall has some intricately patterned plasterwork and is hung with banners, and the Long Gallery has a library containing 5000 books. A superb Chinese Room has recently been restored and is open to the public.

Inside the house is a collection of paintings, and some furniture created by Thomas Chippendale. Housed in the stables visitors will find a museum containing scientific instruments collected in the 18th century by William Constable, and some agricultural machinery and vintage motorcycles.

In summer the grounds are frequently used for traction-engine rallies and light aircraft displays. There are also camping and caravan sites, a picnic area, a children's playground and a model railway.

In the summer the hall is open on weekend afternoons and the grounds are open each afternoon.

Burton Constable Hall is one of the magnificent Tudor architectural glories of Humberside.

The Staircase Hall, Burton Constable.

RIEVAULX ABBEY
near Helmsley, North Yorkshire

Situated in the densely wooded Rye Valley, Rievaulx Abbey is one of the most extensive ruins in England. It was a fine example of early English building and included flying buttresses, three-tiered walls and arcades of pointed arches.

The abbey was founded in 1132 by Cistercian monks, and was once home to Ailred, the third abbot at Rievaulx and spokesman for the Cistercian movement, who made it a place where the weak could come for succour. At the height of its popularity the abbey housed 140 monks and over 500 lay brothers.

Indeed, the monks were ambitious to promote their order and being skilled in farming, wool production and manufacturing crafts created great wealth. At the exhibition in the Visitor Centre the prosperity of this community is illustrated.

The abbey is surrounded by the Yorkshire hills and present-day visitors can follow the hill path leading to the half-mile long Rievaulx Terrace which was created in the 18th century by Thomas Duncombe. Here breathtaking views of the ruins, Ryedale and Hambleton Hills can be seen. Each end of the terrace is marked with a classical temple, a Tuscan rotunda and an Ionic Temple.

Rievaulx Abbey's hauntingly beautiful ruins are amongst the most extensive in England.

NATIONAL MUSEUM OF FILM, PHOTOGRAPHY & TELEVISION
Bradford, West Yorkshire

The National Museum of Film, Photography & Television at Bradford not only follows the development of the media from its earliest beginnings to the latest in satellite technology, but also allows visitors to participate in the fascinating world of the media.

Visitors can see how movement, colour and sound work together in the cinema, and by photography and electronics can explore the workings of a camera.

There are exhibitions of work by major photographers from past masters to present-day professionals. Visitors can try their skills at operating television cameras and can discover the secrets of special effects. There are talks and workshops held by expert photographers and film makers and a newspaper section equipped with telephones on which press photographers recall important moments in their careers. Also on display are historical portrait sittings which include reconstructions of studios in the 1870s and 1930s.

A highlight of the museum is the IMAX cinema where visitors can see films on a screen over 53 feet high and over 63 feet wide. These films include *On the Wing*, which plots the development of flight in insects, birds and man; and *The Dream is Alive*, which follows the lift-off of America's space shuttle and shows astronauts working inside and outside the shuttle.

MOTHER SHIPTON'S CAVE
Knaresborough, North Yorkshire

Mother Shipton was born in Yorkshire over 500 years ago in a cave near Knaresborough's Petrifying Well. When she was born lightning forked the sky, burning her and making her ugly and deformed. At first she was rejected by society but later, as her prophesies increased her fame, she became England's most respected prophetess.

Visitors can trace back the history of the media and participate in this enthralling world at the National Museum of Film, Photography and Television.

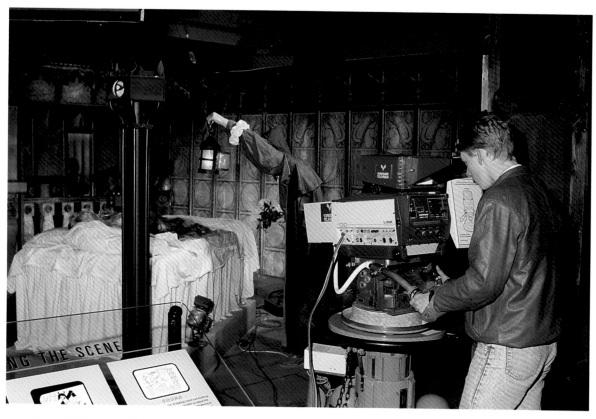

Her predictions included Henry VIII's famous victory against the French, and the invasion and retreat of the Spanish Armada. Mother Shipton is mentioned by Samuel Pepys in his diary which records her warning of the Great Fire of London in 1666. She also foretold the invention of cars, trains, radio and iron ships.

The Petrifying Well which lies next to Mother Shipton's cave is a geological phenomenon. The water that drops from the well contains lime which is gradually changing some everyday objects to stone.

The well and cave were part of the Ancient Forest of Knaresborough and the Nidd Gorge. The riverside walks and carriage drive of the park were classically landscaped with beech trees in the 18th century.

The park is open every day from Easter to October.

Eden Camp Museum
Malton, North Yorkshire

Eden Camp is an award-winning museum and the only modern history theme museum of its kind in the world. Visitors to the museum can experience the sights, sounds and smells of the war years in a reconstructed scene-by-scene museum.

The scenes are created in huts which follow the rise of Hitler and the Nazi party, the declaration of war and the sounds of the 40s, the forming of the home guard, propaganda, the evacuation, and the German U-boat. On display are the tea wagons, the WVS Field Kitchen, and a Red Cross First Aid post. Exhibits also include the fashions of the 40s, a war news room, and a forces re-union hut.

The museum has been constructed from a genuine prisoner-of-war camp and incorporates a junior assault course. It includes an arcade of shops, a souvenir shop and a 'Prisoners Canteen'. There are also daily performances at the puppet show.

The camp is situated off the A64 York to Scarborough road at the Pickering Junction

and is open daily, but visitors are warned they should allow at least two to three hours for a visit.

Lightwater Valley Theme Park
North Stainley, Ripon, North Yorkshire

Set beside 'Herriot' country and the Yorkshire Dales, the Lightwater Valley Theme Park at North Stainley near Ripon is the largest of its kind in the North of England. The park has over 70 rides including Britain's only double loop rollercoaster which towers 80 feet above the ground and the 'Rat', a ride that plunges far underground at top speed through dark sewers that are alive with the sound of rats.

The park has been open for ten years and is set in 125 acres of parkland where visitors can stroll and enjoy the lakes, flora and fauna and birds and animals. There is a miniature steam railway, a grand prix racing track, and boating lake. Within the grounds is a unique and award-winning farm. Here, from carpeted walkways, visitors can view modern farming methods, watch chicks hatching and sows with their piglets, and see the only visitors' snail farm in the world.

On a quieter note the park has a bowling green, an old time fair, sandpits, swings and slides and a nine hole par three golf course. There is also a traditional 'olde worlde' shopping street and a market square.

Castle Howard
near York, North Yorkshire

Castle Howard was built for Charles Howard in 1700 to replace Henderskelfe Castle which had been burned down in 1639 and is still owned by the family today. It was designed by architect Sir John Vanbrugh who was aided by Nicholas Hawksmoor – one of Sir Christopher Wren's assistants. Present-day

Castle Howard, with its abundance of opulence and splendour, was the first building designed by Vanbrugh.

visitors may well experience a sense of *déjà vu* on entering the house and grounds as Castle Howard was the setting for much of the acclaimed television series 'Brideshead Revisited'.

The Red Dining Room, Castle Howard.

Castle Howard is set in magnificent grounds which include parkland, rose gardens and nature walks.

The central block is surmounted by a huge domed roof and long before visitors reach the castle this can be seen above the trees. This imposing exterior is matched only by the lavish interior. The great hall is 70 feet high and 34 feet square, and has a domed ceiling. The rooms are hung with paintings by Rubens, Gainsborough, Reynolds and Holbein, and contain statues from ancient Greece and Rome.

The house is set in thousands of acres of parklands with nature walks, beautiful rose gardens and a plant centre. The grounds also house the Temple of the Four Winds and the Mausoleum which was designed by Vanbrugh and completed by Hawksmoor. In a building adjacent to the house is a Costume Gallery displaying costumes from the 17th–20th centuries.

The house and gardens are open daily during the spring and summer.

YORKSHIRE MINING MUSEUM
Overton, Wakefield

The Yorkshire Mining Museum is located on the A642 between Huddersfield and Wakefield and illustrates to visitors the harsh reality of coal mining which began in Britain in Roman times on a small scale until the industrial revolution brought a boom to the industry.

The museum includes a real mine and visitors are taken on an underground tour, but are advised to wear thick clothing and sensible shoes as the mine is very cold. Children under five are not allowed underground.

The museum also includes an audio-visual theatre depicting mining through the ages. Here visitors can see the surface machinery used to sort the coal, real pit ponies – bred for their small stature which is well suited for the mines – and the paddy trains used to transport the coal from the face to the shaft. Visitors can see the steam winding house and view the many exhibits of the industry in the indoor exhibition area.

The museum is open daily throughout the year – excluding Christmas Day and New Year's Day – from 10am to 5pm.

Visitors can see the underground working of a typical coal mine at the Yorkshire Mining Museum.

YORK

As the principal garrison in Roman Britain, York was for many years regarded as the northern capital. It remained under Roman occupation for 340 years until the Saxons took over and made it a centre of learning. York was later captured by the Danes and occupied by Normans. In 1069 a fire enabled the Normans to build a new town five times larger and York became a major fortress as well as a wool centre. It was during this time that the construction of York Minster began. The construction of this imposing building took 250 years, and today it is the largest Gothic church in England and still dominates the city.

York's prosperity declined with the wool industry until the 18th century when there was a revival. This prosperity was hastened in the 19th century when York became the great railway centre that it is today. As well as being an industrial centre for the manufacture of sugar, glass, and railway engineering, York is an important market town, and an educational and major tourist centre.

Tourist attractions include the Viking City of Jorvik, the ancient city which was unearthed beneath Coppergate by archaeologists in the 1970s. They found beneath present-day streets, complete 10th-century houses and workshops which still contain the utensils, tools and clothing buried centuries ago. These can be seen replaced exactly where they were found. The centre also has 'time cars' which take visitors back to a bustling market, smokey houses and a busy wharf of Viking Britain.

Petergate, York.

YORK

York is the cultural capital of the north of England and still a bustling market town. York railway station (top, left); the Jorvik Viking Centre (above); The Shambles (above, right); a fireguard plaque (centre); and Clifford's Tower (below).

As an ancient walled city, York has a wealth of buildings of historic interest. These include York Minster, where visitors can view more than half of England's remaining medieval stained glass; the Castle Museum housed in two classical 18th-century prisons and containing reconstructions of streets and shops from Tudor to Victorian times; King's Manor — once home of the Abbot of St Mary's Abbey; the National Railway Museum; York Castle, where the Clifford's Tower is all that remains of the Norman Castle; the York Story — a heritage centre containing audiovisual displays and exhibitions of crafts; and Yorkshire Museum and Gardens exhibiting a Roman, medieval and natural history collection.

York Minster took 250 years to build.

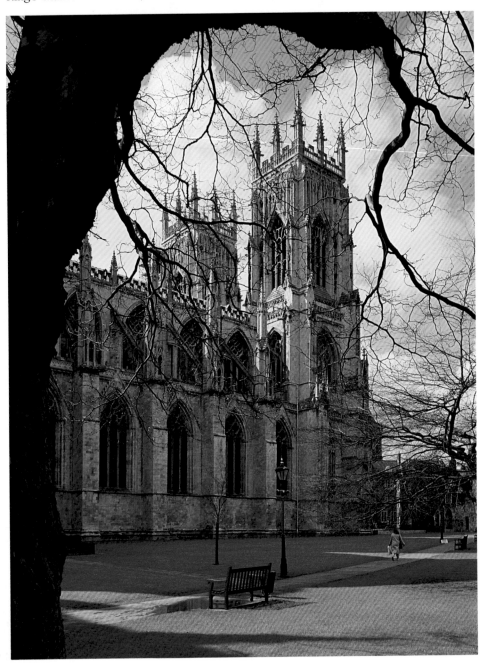

Beggar's Bridge at Glaisdale, built by a poor local boy to facilitate his journey across the river to court his beloved one.

ESK VALLEY

Home to Captain James Cook the Esk Valley runs through 35 miles of valley villages to the sea at Whitby.

The trail begins at Middlesbrough and the Cleveland shopping centre, where, suspended in the main hall, visitors can see a 22 foot model of Captain Cook's famous ship, the 'Endeavour'.

Next stop is Marton, where attractions include the Captain Cook Birthplace Museum at Stewart Park. Here can be found a conservatory containing rare plants brought home by Cook's botanists, recreated historic scenes and a children's zoo. Opposite the park is Tennis World, one of Britain's most advanced tennis centres.

At Great Ayton is Cook's old schoolhouse which is now a museum, and set on the slopes of Roseberry Topping and towering 1000 feet above the village is the farm where he once lived.

Danby is the centre of one of Britain's largest national parks which measures 553 square miles. While at Lealholm the river breaks over rocky falls, and visitors can cross the water either by stepping stones or by using the 200-year-old stone bridge.

Glaisdale — once home of three smelting furnaces — today is more famous for its Beggar's Bridge built in 1619. The story follows that a poor local boy had to wade across the river to court the squire's daughter, and when he was turned away, went off to make his fortune. When he returned to marry his love he built the bridge to keep other travellers dry.

Further along the line is Egton where every August since 1800 a Gooseberry Show has been held, while at Grosmont visitors can board the steam train and travel back to the year 1865 when steam trains ran across the moors between Pickering and Whitby.

The river Esk is Yorkshire's only salmon river and sometimes further along the line at Sleights, salmon can be seen leaping up the river.

Whitby is the end of the line where Captain Cook's statue stands on the West Cliff overlooking the fishing harbour.

SPURN HEAD Holderness

Spurn Head is a nature reserve run by the Yorkshire Wildlife Trust. It is situated at the southern tip of Holderness and was formed by sand and shingle washed by the sea from the cliffs.

The head comprises of acres of mud flats that are uncovered at low tide. It is a popular area for birdwatchers who come to see the enormous variety of birds inhabiting the reserve. These include dunlin, wheatear, winchats, redstarts, pied and spotted fly-catchers, oystercatchers, terns, curlews and, during the winter months, the Brent Geese. Indeed the reserve is one of Europe's major points for observing bird migration. It is also a favourite haunt of seals who can some-times be seen basking on the sandbanks, and occasionally porpoises are viewed off-shore.

Visitors can drive along the Head which has views on one side stretching along the Humber and the distant Lincolnshire coast, and on the other the North Sea. Cargo ships can be seen queueing to enter the estuary and occasionally traditional vessels such as the Humber keel 'Comrade' or her sister ship the Humber sloop 'Amy Howson', can be seen.

Almost at the tip of the Head stands a lighthouse built in the late 19th century. The tip itself is closed to the public, but at low tide visitors can walk around by beaches where corals and ammonites can be found — but visitors should remember to beware of changing tides.

The reserve is situated nine miles south-east of Patrington and is open daily throughout the year.

BOLTON CASTLE
Wensleydale, North Yorkshire

The busy harbour and marine parade at Whitby (right).

Bolton Castle was built by Richard le Scrope – the Lord Chancellor of England to Richard II – in the 14th century. In 1568-9 it was the prison of Mary, Queen of Scots who was imprisoned by her cousin Elizabeth I because of her embarrassing claim to the British throne. Mary was used as the figure head of many plots to oust Elizabeth and eventually she was executed at Fother-inghay Castle near Peterborough.

The castle is said to be escape-proof, and the walls were reputedly built with ox blood mixed with mortar for added strength; nevertheless, it is claimed that Mary escaped through a window but was soon recaptured.

The original banqueting hall now houses a restaurant. Also of interest is the great chamber with exposed beams, and the Mary Queen of Scots bed chamber. There is also a horse mill.

The castle is open daily from March to mid November, and is situated between Carperby and Redmire. Nearby is an estate village named Castle Bolton which has a beautiful medieval church where exhibitions are often held.

WHITBY North Yorkshire

Whitby is situated at the picturesque mouth of the river Esk. It is a holiday resort and for hundreds of years has been a fishing port. A mark of this heritage is the terrace of fisher-men's cottages standing beneath East Cliff.

Whitby has been a fishing port for centuries.

The history of Whitby dates back to AD 657 when a monastery was founded by St Hilda. In 664 the Synod of Whitby met here and the divided Church of England decided to accept the authority of the Roman Catholic Church. Later, in the 7th century, the monastery became home to Caedmon, the monk who wrote the first Christian poem. It is claimed this poem marked the beginning of English literature. Today in St Mary's Church stands a commemorative cross dedicated to Caedmon.

The ruins of Whitby Abbey are reached by 199 steps and command magnificent views over the town. These remains are not of the original monastery but belong to a later 13th-century building.

Whitby reached the height of its prosperity in the 18th century when it had a whaling fleet and was a base for coalships. As a young boy, Captain James Cook ran away to Whitby, and he worked and learnt the trade which was to take him around the world on these ships. He remained in Whitby for nine years, and a plaque marks the house where he lived in Grape Lane. The 'Endeavour' and the 'Resolution', the ships he commanded, were built locally.

Places of interest include Pannett Park where exhibits include a large display of fossils, and a section devoted to Captain Cook and where Cook's handwritten survey of Placentia Bay, Newfoundland is exhibited. In the local history section visitors will find the 'Tempest Prognosticator' – an instrument which forecasts thunderstorms – which once belonged to Dr Merryweather.

Other entertainments include the Whitby festival held in June which is a fortnight of events that draw together local talent in the performing arts; the Angling Festival held in July which is an event for both the serious and amateur angler; the Riva Cup Race – a yacht race held in early August – which comprises of a regatta at sea and a carnival on land; and the Whitby Folk Festival.

HAREWOOD HOUSE Leeds

Harewood House was built by John Carr in 1759, for Edwin Lascelles who had settled in Yorkshire after the Norman Conquest. Later it became home to HRH Princess Royal, the daughter of King George V, who remained there until her death in 1965. Harewood, which lies seven miles north of Leeds, is now home to the Earl and Countess of Harewood.

The house was decorated by Robert Adam and furnished by Thomas Chippendale. This furniture has become the richest collection of Chippendale in the world. Inside there are

The library at Harewood House provides more of interest than books, with its ornate Adam ceiling and Yorkshire landscapes by Turner.

Adam ceilings and art of international renown including paintings by artist John Singer Sargent, Epstein's famous *Adam*, and some Sèvres and Chinese porcelain.

Capability Brown was commissioned to design the surrounding parkland in 1772, and he worked for nine years to create 30 acres of woodland walks, lakeside views and herbaceous borders – the terraces present today were a later addition. The Princess Royal planted rhododendrons in the gardens and today the grounds contain over 100 different species. There is also an adventure playground constructed of Harewood timber and designed by Leeds School of Landscape Architecture and this is suitable for both children and adults.

The grounds incorporate a four acre bird garden containing a collection of exotic and endangered species, ranging from the emu to the humming bird. An extension of the bird garden is the Tropical Rain Forest exhibition which allows visitors to experience the conditions of the climate in a simulated section of rain forest. The vegetation, birds and reptiles are as near to authenticity as possible.

FOR FURTHER INFORMATION CONTACT:

Tourist Information Centre
King George Dock
Hedon Road
HULL
Humberside HU9 5PR
Telephone: (0482) 702118

Tourist Information Centre
19 Wellington Street
LEEDS
West Yorkshire LS1 4DG
Telephone: (0532) 462454/5

Tourist Information Centre
De Grey Rooms
Exhibition Square
YORK
North Yorkshire YO1 2HB
Telephone: (0904) 621756/7

Yorkshire & Humberside Tourist Board
213 Tadcaster Road
YORK
North Yorkshire YO2 2HF
Telephone: (0904) 707961

CUMBRIA

Levens Hall, Cumbria.

Cumbria is a land of rugged mountains, forests and deep lakes, farmland, scattered villages and an abundance of wildlife. The area includes the Lake District which is flanked on one side by the Pennines and on the other by the coast.

The forests are home to the red squirrel, red deer and roe deer, and badgers – although these are in limited numbers now. Mud flats sprawl along the endless coastline, providing a home to the rare natterjack toads, eider duck, oyster-catchers, turnstones, the largest colony of blackheaded gulls in England and a variety of terns. Fish such as the fluke, plaice and sea food such as mussels and shrimps also find their haven here. The lakes, too, support a variety of fish including the rare schelly, a fish sometimes called the fresh water herring, and the char, an alpine relative of the trout that can only survive in waters below 15°C.

As well as natural geological beauty, Cumbria's social history has tended towards turbulence and bloodiness. The land has been the site of viking raids, feudal battles and fights between the English and Scottish thrones who were constantly battling for supremacy in the area. Relics of past fortifications include Hardknott Fort and Dalton Castle.

The wild landscape has been home to many religious orders, some of whom were given land by Norman barons eager to gain favour with the Almighty. Religion still thrives in the area and during July Keswick hosts the religious convention.

The climate is an ever changing and often tough one, which varies from valley to valley. Local industries once included sheep and dairy farming, mining, forestry and iron smelting. Today the area is still agricultural, and the forestry trade continues, but coal supplies are almost exhausted although the land is still mined for granite and limestone. New industries include the chemical industry.

For centuries the beauty of the area has inspired poets and writers such as William Wordsworth who speaks of the Lakeland in many of his poems, and Beatrix Potter whose writing and drawings depict her intimate knowledge of the wildlife of her childhood.

Cumbria was once a centre for the spice trade and culinary specialities include the spicy Cumberland sausage, and Cumberland sauce. There is also a wealth of natural foods such as fresh shrimps, muscles, smoked trout and char, which is a delicacy of the area.

Despite tourism, under the control of the Lake District National Park – the largest landowner in the county – the area has remained unspoilt, and largely true to its natural beauty.

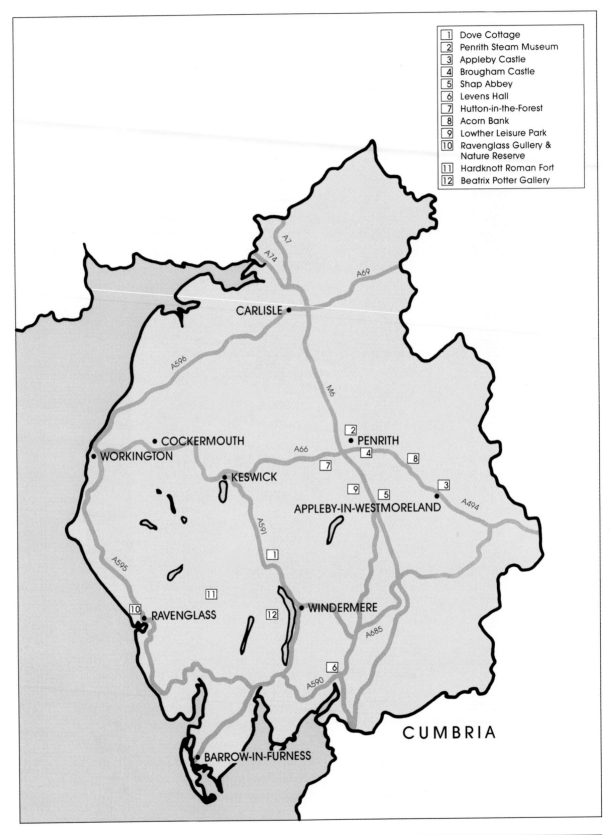

1	Dove Cottage
2	Penrith Steam Museum
3	Appleby Castle
4	Brougham Castle
5	Shap Abbey
6	Levens Hall
7	Hutton-in-the-Forest
8	Acorn Bank
9	Lowther Leisure Park
10	Ravenglass Gullery & Nature Reserve
11	Hardknott Roman Fort
12	Beatrix Potter Gallery

CARLISLE

COCKERMOUTH

WORKINGTON

KESWICK

PENRITH

APPLEBY-IN-WESTMORELAND

RAVENGLASS

WINDERMERE

BARROW-IN-FURNESS

CUMBRIA

HARDKNOTT ROMAN FORT

Hardknott Fort is a vast stone fort which was built by the Romans to protect the road from Ambleside to the Roman port at Ravenglass. It is set on a high shelf and is reached by the Hardknott Pass – a single-track 1 in 3 gradient road. The Fort commands excellent views and on a clear day visitors can see across the Scafell range, and the Eskdale valley to the distant Isle of Man.

During Roman times the fort was called Mediobogdum and an inscription inside confirms it was rebuilt during Hadrian's reign. The fort covers three acres of land yet it is easy to bypass without being aware of its existence; there is no road sign, and only a small car park cut in the bank indicates the fort which lies behind.

The fort is set on a sloping plateau and the outer wall which has been partly restored by the Department of the Environment still stands ten feet high. The site comprises of sheer rock and the labour required to level it must have been tremendous. The foundations of the headquarters building, the commander's house and the granary can still be clearly defined. There is also a parade ground nearby to the east where Roman troops were once paraded.

The fort's attraction lies in the knowledge that the view of the mountain clouds, the surrounding farmland and the sound of the wind battering against the crags must have remained unchanged since Roman times.

ACORN BANK GARDEN
Temple Sowerby, near Penrith, Cumbria

Acorn Bank Garden was bequeathed to the National Trust in 1950. It lies to the north of Temple Sowerby and is a 2½ acre garden surrounded by wide oak trees. In spring the garden is a blaze of colour with daffodils and narcissi in full bloom.

Acorn Bank's chief claim to fame is its herb garden. The garden contains over 250 varieties of medieval culinary and medicinal herbs, making it the most extensive herb garden in the north. Many of these herbs are rare plants.

The gardens also contain some unusual trees and in the two walled orchards there

Hardknott Roman Fort was called Mediobogdum by the Romans, meaning 'in the middle of a bend in the river'.

are wild fruit trees including bird cherry and crab apple. Surrounding the orchard is a well-stocked garden containing shrubs, herbaceous plants and roses. There is also a greenhouse which has recently been restored.

Standing in the gardens is a 17th- to 18th-century red sandstone house which is let to the Sue Ryder Foundation. Admission to the house is available on application to the trust.

The gardens are open daily from April to November.

DOVE COTTAGE *Grasmere, Cumbria*

Today Dove Cottage is an award-winning museum, but it was once a place of literary repute. Its most famous literary occupant was William Wordsworth who lived here with his sister from 1799 to 1808. During this time he wrote many of his most noted poems, including *The Prelude* and *Intimations of Immortality.*

The home of the poet Wordsworth is now an award-winning museum with unique memorabilia devoted to Wordsworth and the Romantic movement.

The cottage at Grasmere is owned by the Wordsworth Trust who bought it in 1890. The aim of the trust is to conserve the unique collection of memorabilia devoted to Wordsworth and the Romantic movement.

Details of Wordsworth's life at Dove Cottage can be found in his sister Dorothy's journals and some of these are on display. Recorded in the journals are frequent visits of other famous authors including Thomas De Quincey, Sir Walter Scott and Samuel Taylor Coleridge. Thomas De Quincey also occupied the house after the Wordsworths left, and he too wrote much of his most noted work here.

The cottage still contains some of Wordsworth's furniture and looks much as it would have done during his occupation. Other exhibits include a reconstructed 19th-century farm kitchen, a display of Wordsworth's early notes and manuscripts and some portraits and paintings.

Visitors can have a guided tour of the cottage and view the garden, 'a little nook of mountain ground', which is open in fine weather. There is also a restaurant providing meals and snacks throughout the day.

BROUGHAM CASTLE
Brougham, near Penrith, Cumbria

Brougham Castle is situated south east of Penrith and is an impressive ruin of a moated Norman Keep. The castle stands by the River Eamont near an arched bridge spanning the river. It was built close to an earlier Roman fort called Brocavum which can be viewed to the south.

The castle was added to in the 13th century by Robert Clifford and was restored in the 17th century by Lady Anne Clifford.

Visitors enter the castle by the outer gatehouse. Here the inscription 'thys made Roger' can be seen, referring to the fifth Lord Clifford. Another inscription in the gate hall records the structural repairs begun in 1651 by Lady Anne. These alterations made the castle inhabitable and it was here that Lady Anne spent her remaining years until 1676 when she died, aged 86, in the bedroom where her father had been born.

The Great Chamber is in ruins now but the keep is well preserved and contains interesting detail. Present-day visitors can climb a spiral staircase and take a bird's eye view of the impressive remains. The hall, kitchen, chapel and lodgings are still intact and the south-west tower, the Tower of League – a three-storey building built in the 13th century by Robert Clifford – is also still standing.

SHAP ABBEY Shap, Cumbria

Shap Abbey was founded at Preston Patrick in about 1180 and was moved to Shap in 1199. It stands one mile to the west of Shap Fell – which at over 1000 feet is the highest point on the A6 – in a secluded valley by the River Lowther. The abbey belonged to the 'white canons', monastic canons of the Premonstratensian Order who always wore white clothing.

The abbey has some 13th- and 14th-century additions and stood until the dissolution in 1534. A striking feature is the tower of the abbey church which stands to almost its full height.

The church plan can be clearly defined and some of the later 13th-century buildings are standing. There is some 14th-century vaulting and the cellars which once stood beneath the refectory can still be seen.

Close to the abbey lies the 'Thunder Stone' which forms part of a prehistoric standing stone circle. To the south is Keld, a hamlet with a 16th-century chapel belonging to the National Trust.

Admission is free and the abbey is open at any reasonable time.

BEATRIX POTTER GALLERY
Hawkshead, Cumbria

The Beatrix Potter Gallery is a newly created exhibition at Hawkshead. The gallery exhibits a selection of Beatrix Potter's original drawings and illustrations from her children's story books including Peter Rabbit – the first of her books to be published in 1900. The display will change annually.

The exhibition tells the story of her life as an author, artist, farmer and preserver of the Lake District. There is a cabinet of farming trophies and pictures from her famous stories created from her childhood observation of animals.

The gallery is set in the building which was once the office of her solicitor husband, William Heelis early this century, and it remains mostly unchanged.

Hawkshead contains several literary landmarks. The grammar school had as a pupil the young William Wordsworth and several 17th-century buildings in two ancient squares in the village are now in the care of the National Trust to whom they

The Beatrix Potter Gallery hosts an exhibition which tells the story of the much loved writer's life.

were donated by Beatrix Potter.

The gallery is open from April to November from Monday to Friday and weekends during February and March.

LOWTHER LEISURE PARK
Hackthorpe, near Penrith, Cumbria

The Lowther Leisure Park of Hackthorpe near Penrith, contains over 40 attractions, including Stevenson's Crown Circus. The circus performances take place daily during April and from the end of May to the beginning of September. The circus comprises a 50 minute show of international acts including animal acts from Mary Chipper-

Visitors never have a dull moment at Lowther Leisure Park, which has over 40 attractions.

field's stable, trapeze acts and trick cycling. Some of the artists are of international repute and have performed in command performances.

Lowther Leisure Park covers 150 acres, and is part of an ancient deer park which was granted to Sir Hugh Lowther in 1283 by Edward I. Red deer can still be seen roaming the park and the animals of this herd are the direct descendants of those medieval beasts.

The undulating parkland and woodland attracts a wide variety of birds and animals, and visitors to the park can enjoy nature walks through beautiful unspoilt land. The park is also home to peacocks and macaws and wild water fowl.

Other attractions include a nine hole pitch and putt course, an astra glide and a covered archery range. There is also a boating lake, steam train, climbing frames, a tin can alley, football and netball areas, ten pin bowling, roller skating, wobbly boards, a giant sandpit, aerial cableways and a tarzan trail assault course.

Visitors to the park pay on admittance and this fee includes the circus.

RAVENGLASS GULLERY AND NATURE RESERVE *Ravenglass, Cumbria*

Ravenglass Gullery and Nature Reserve is a must for nature lovers. Situated on the west coast on the Drigg dunes, the stretch of sands forming the reserve supports a wealth of birds. It is also the breeding ground for the Natterjack toad – Britain's rarest amphibian – which is distinguished by a yellow line running down its head and back and by its loud voice.

The reserve is owned by Muncaster Castle and managed by Cumbria County Council. It has the largest colony of black-headed gulls in England and is the breeding ground for birds including shelduck, red breasted merganser, ringed plover, sandwich, and common and arctic terns.

Drigg can be located off the A595 north of Ravenglass which stands on the other side of the estuary.

KESWICK *Cumbria*

Keswick was once a small mining town, but since Victorian times has been a tourist centre. Most of the main buildings date from this period and Moot Hall, situated in the main square, was built in 1813. The oldest building in the town is the parish church of Crosthwaite. Part of the church is believed to date from the 12th century.

The town has a small museum in a large public park, containing a mineral section and letters and writing from some of the many writers who have found inspiration in this area of overwhelming natural beauty.

To the south west of the town lies Derwent water. In the centre of the lake is the island where St Herbert established a hermitage in AD 685. It is claimed that the remains of the monk's cell can still be seen beneath the dense undergrowth. Visitors can explore the lake and its islands either by boarding a scheduled Keswick Launch, or in a rowing boat or self-drive motor launch.

Other attractions include the Keswick

Keswick seen from Hawes.

Railway Museum on Main Street; housed in the closed station the museum incorporates an exhibition of local railway photographs and an operating model railway. The Motor Museum at Standish Street features famous celebrity television and film vehicles, and the Pencil Museum exhibits include the world's first pencils and displays of the history of graphite mining in Borrowdale.

KENDAL *Cumbria*

The town of Kendal, with its many limestone buildings that bestowed upon it the name of the 'auld grey town', is the administrative capital and largest town of the Lake District.

Kendal was established as a woollen-weaving industry in 1331 when Flemish weavers settled here, giving rise to the town's motto 'Pannus mihi panis' – 'wool is my bread'.

There are a wealth of fascinating buildings to visit: the ruined Norman castle which was the birthplace of Catherine Parr, Henry VIII's sixth wife, overlooks the Lake District National Park; the Abbot Hall Art Gallery is a magnificent 18th-century mansion with a collection of superb paintings, and its stables house the Museum of Lakeland Life and Industry; and the relatively new town hall has a carillon in its tower which plays English, Welsh, Scottish and Irish tunes – mercifully only six times a day.

KENDAL

Kendal parish church (above, left); Abbot Hall Art Gallery (top, right); view of the town from Castle Hill (above); site of the Roman Fort (left); and the bridge at Kendal (below).

HUTTON-IN-THE-FOREST
Penrith, Cumbria

Legend claims Lord Inglewood's house at Hutton-in-the-Forest was the site of the Green Knight's castle in the Arthurian tales of Sir Gawain and the Green Knight. Today the house is home to Lord and Lady Inglewood and their children and has belonged to the family since 1600.

The medieval peel tower is the oldest part of the house; the remainder dates from a variety of periods as almost every generation of the family has made additions to create a very unusual and interesting house.

A Cupid staircase – named after its cherub carvings – dominates the 17th-century Hall. The Gallery, which dates from 1630, is a rare feature in a northern house and contains a fine collection of furniture and portraits. A more recent addition – a Victorian Drawing Room – is a reminder of a leisurely way of life now long gone. The Cupid Room which has been restored and redecorated, incorporates a beautiful plaster ceiling.

The house lies in woodland of the medi-eval forest of Inglewood. The Walled Gardens were built in 1730 and include a variety of flowers and plants. The 17th-century Topiary Terraces round the house are the foundation for the Victorian woodland garden which contains specimen trees and leads to the largest of the ornamental ponds.

The house is open to the public from Easter to September. Each Friday afternoon from June to September, visitors can attend lectures which feature themes ranging from the appreciation of tapestries, gardening and housekeeping to advice on herbs and potions. On Thursday afternoons during August there is a dramatic tour of the house with a treasure hunt and quiz for children, but this must be booked in advance.

LEVENS HALL Kendal, Cumbria

Levens Hall is situated five miles south of Kendal and is an Elizabethan mansion developed from a 13th-century defensive peel tower that once belonged to the de Redmans family. In the 16th century the house was sold to James Bellingham who extended and

The Topiary Gardens at Levens Hall have been carefully tended for three centuries.

improved it, but later it was lost in gambling debts by James Bellingham's grandson and taken over by James Graham. It was under his authority that Monsieur Beaumont – a gardener of high repute who was much sought after by the gentry – was hired to create the famous gardens.

From 1690 to his death in 1730 Monsieur Beaumont worked on the gardens to create an unusual topiary garden of yew trees cut in a variety of shapes. Today the topiary garden remains almost unchanged. The garden also contains a variety of colourful as well as unusual plants.

From James Graham the house passed by marriage to Henry Bowes Howard then again by marriage to the Bagots, who are the present owners. Inside is a collection of Jacobean furniture, a panelled interior, intricate plasterwork and paintings. Cordova leather wall coverings dating from the 17th century grace the walls and the earliest English patchwork is also exhibited.

There is a fine collection of working model steam engines and most Sundays and bank holiday Mondays visitors can see working traction engines.

LEEDS – SETTLE – CARLISLE LINE

Memorable and thrilling are words that best describe the 70 miles rail link from Leeds to Carlisle. The line takes passengers from the historic cities of West Yorkshire, via the picturesque Yorkshire Dales, over the Pennines, into the Eden Valley and onto historic Carlisle, through an ever changing and still unspoilt countryside.

Reputedly one of the most memorable journeys in the world, passengers cross lonely moors, valleys, and mountains on lines, viaducts, bridges and tunnels built by hand over 120 years ago. This fine example of Victorian engineering allowed both Victorian, and now present-day walkers and climbers access to hitherto untrampled countryside.

Steam traction engines and vintage farm machinery are on view at Penrith Steam Museum.

Close to the line runs the 250 mile Pennine-way footpath, the River Ribble and the Ingleborough and Pen-y-Ghent peaks. The trains stop at Leeds, where passengers can visit Kirkstall Abbey, Armley Mill, the Tropical World, and Roundhay Park; Bradford where attractions include the Alhambra Theatre, and the National Museum of Photography, Film and Television; and Saltaire which is Sir Titus Salt's Ideal Village; other stops include Bingley, Keighley, Settle, Garsdale, and Appleby-In-Westmorland.

From Horton-in-Ribblesdale the line climbs north by the Ribblehead 24-arch viaduct to Dent, the highest main line station in England. Then passengers are taken into the beautiful Eden Valley and on to Carlisle, either to simply relax, or follow the City Centre Trail to the Norman castle and 12th-century cathedral which is the third oldest in the north.

PENRITH STEAM MUSEUM
Penrith, Cumbria

Penrith Steam Museum is a working museum of steam traction engines and vintage farm machinery. The museum includes a blacksmith working iron in the forge, a pattern shop and steam models. Present-day visitors can also step back into the past and view the frugal existence of a furnished Victorian cottage.

The museum is situated close to the town centre of Penrith near the main railway station. Penrith is a market town built of red sandstone and is the main gateway to the Lake District. It has been a central point for travellers since the Bronze age and visitors can climb Penrith Beacon which was once used as a communication point, and on clear days provides excellent views across the country.

The museum is open during the Easter weekend and from Whitsun to the end of September, Mondays to Fridays. It is also open on bank holiday weekends and provides an excellent day trip on wet days as the displays are under cover.

Trumpeter Swans (above, right) live in leisurely style at Appleby Castle's Conservation Centre (above), which is the centre of the Rare Breeds Survival Trust.

APPLEBY CASTLE AND CONSERVATION CENTRE
Appleby-in-Westmorland, Cumbria

Appleby Castle is not just a fascinating relic of bygone days, but a modern conservation centre. As a centre for the Rare Breeds Survival Trust, the riverside grounds are home to many rare British farm animals. A collection of waterfowl, pheasants, poultry, owls, finches and parakeets can be found in the beautifully arranged gardens which are open to the public from Easter to the end of September.

As well as the grounds, present-day visitors have access to all floors of the castle. The Norman Keep dates back to 1100, while the tower is a 13th-century addition. The castle was almost destroyed by Cromwell, but was rebuilt in 1653 by Lady Anne Clifford who, in defiance of Cromwell, made the restoration and improvement of her family's estates and houses her life's work.

Exhibits include Roman armour and insignia, medieval furniture, decorated shields – made by historians closely following the style they believed was prevalent in medieval times – 17th-century household furniture, and a rare collection of early 19th-century bikes. Paintings depicting country activities during the four seasons also reveal something of life during a bygone era.

The Great Hall of the house is also open to the public and incorporates the 'Great Picture', which is a triptych painted in 1646 of the Clifford Family. Other items on display include a Chinese porcelain dinner service, salvaged in 1986 with other household effects from the Nanking Cargo which had been resting 130 feet below the South China Sea since 1752.

FOR FURTHER INFORMATION CONTACT:

Tourist Information Centre
Old Town Hall
Green Market
CARLISLE
Cumbria CA3 8JH
Telephone: (0228) 25517

Tourist Information Centre
Moot Hall
Market Square
KESWICK
Cumbria CA12 5JR
Telephone: (07687) 74101

Cumbria Tourist Board
Ashleigh
Holly Road
WINDERMERE LA23 2AQ
Telephone: (09662) 4444

NORTHUMBRIA

The River Wear, overlooked by Durham Cathedral.

Northumbria is made up of England's four most northerly counties – Cleveland, Durham, Tyne & Wear, and Northumberland. It also boasts some of England's finest countryside – the North Pennines' Area of Outstanding Beauty, the Northumberland National Park and the Cleveland Hills – as well as around 100 miles of Heritage Coast.

Because of its isolation, much of Northumbria's countryside remains undiscovered by tourists, yet fast roads bring it within easy reach of centres such as Newcastle-upon-Tyne and Durham. At one time, the North Pennines were the home of thousands employed by the lead-mining industry; now there are more sheep than people even at the height of summer.

The area's turbulent military history has left its mark on the landscape. The remains of Hadrian's Wall snake across some of the wildest countryside in England, and the region boasts more castles and fortified houses than anywhere else in the country. Some (like Bamburgh) are still inhabited while the ruins of others (Dunstanburgh and Warkworth, for example) remain impressive enough to remind visitors of their former grandeur.

Reminders abound, too, of Northumbria's early ecclesiastical importance. Lindisfarne was one of the first centres of Christianity in England, and it is still possible to follow the first pilgrims' route across the causeway to that tiny island and its ruined Norman priory. Durham Cathedral, the Bede Monastery Museum (Jarrow) and St Peter's Church (Monkwearmouth) contain relics of that time. At Escomb (County Durham) is one of the finest surviving Saxon churches in the country; the ruins of Egglestone Abbey and the former priories of Gisborough, Finchale and Brinkburn reflect Northumbria's influence as a place of scholarship and culture.

Northumbria's fishing industry is centuries old. The Marine Life Centre and Fishing Museum at Seahouses concentrates on its development over the past 100 years, and houses the biggest seawater aquarium in the north-east. Along the coast there are still a handful of stunning beaches scattered with tiny fishing villages, though the hundreds of small smokehouses for curing herrings have now gone. The most famous is at Craster, where kippers have been cured in the same way for 150 years.

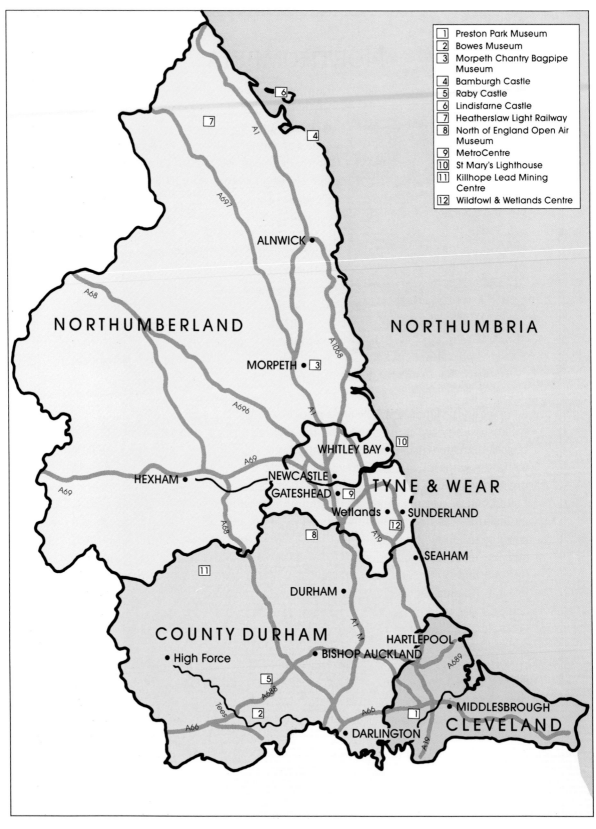

1. Preston Park Museum
2. Bowes Museum
3. Morpeth Chantry Bagpipe Museum
4. Bamburgh Castle
5. Raby Castle
6. Lindisfarne Castle
7. Heatherslaw Light Railway
8. North of England Open Air Museum
9. MetroCentre
10. St Mary's Lighthouse
11. Killhope Lead Mining Centre
12. Wildfowl & Wetlands Centre

NORTHUMBERLAND

NORTHUMBRIA

ALNWICK

MORPETH 3

WHITLEY BAY 10

HEXHAM

NEWCASTLE
GATESHEAD 9

TYNE & WEAR

Wetlands
12 SUNDERLAND

8

SEAHAM

11

DURHAM

COUNTY DURHAM

High Force

BISHOP AUCKLAND

HARTLEPOOL

5

2

MIDDLESBROUGH

DARLINGTON

CLEVELAND

LINDISFARNE CASTLE
Holy Island, Northumberland

Lindisfarne Castle, built in 1550 to protect Holy Island's harbour against marauding Scots, was one of Northumbria's tiniest fortresses. Some of the red sandstone used to build it came from the ruined priory nearby, established by St Aidan in the 7th century but largely destroyed by Danish raiders a century and a half later.

Sir Edwin Lutyens − designer, among other things, of the Cenotaph in London's Whitehall and Liverpool's Roman Catholic Cathedral − restored the castle in 1903 as a private house. It is now in the care of the National Trust, and open to the public between April and the end of September. Its small walled garden was the work of Gertrude Jekyll.

High tide submerges the causeway that links Holy Island to the mainland, racing in rapidly across the sand flats that form part of Holy Island's fine nature reserve. Wildfowl and wading birds feed here; other seabirds inhabit the island's limestone cliffs, and seals are often seen offshore.

Remote, peaceful and mysterious, Holy Island supports a small community of people involved with fishing and tourism.

Mead, a wine made from fermented honey and spices whose existence is recorded in some of the earliest English writings in existence, is still made here.

HADRIAN'S WALL Northumberland

Once the Roman Empire's northern frontier, and still one of its greatest military monuments, Hadrian's Wall marked the boundary between British lands the Romans were able to conquer 2000 years ago and those which steadfastly resisted the advance of 'civilisation'. A garrison of 5,500 cavalry and 13,000 infantry soldiers had the job of guarding the Empire's land from attacks mounted by the northern barbarians, and was stationed along the length of the Wall which spanned the whole width of northern England.

Building began under Hadrian's orders in the year 122. When it was finished − probably within 40 years − the Wall was over 70 miles long. Seventeen forts provided soldiers' accommodation, milecastles every Roman mile were the headquarters for security patrols, and turrets between them acted as observation posts. In time, civilian settlements − complete with houses, bars, workshops and temples − developed around the forts.

Lindisfarne Castle was converted from its original purpose as a 16th-century fortress, into a private house by Sir Edward Lutyens in 1903.

Hadrian's Wall (above) seen from the west of Housesteads Fort.
The Wildfowl and Wetlands Centre (below, left) was created out of nothing less than 20 years ago, and is now open all year round.

Reminders of the Wall, the soldiers who manned it and the settlements that grew up nearby can still be seen. The excavations and museum at Vindolanda, the forts at Chesters and Housesteads, and the settlement at Corbridge are all popular with visitors. Less well-known, though no less evocative, are the Sewingshields wall turrets and milecastle near Haydon Bridge. Not far away is the Carrawburgh Temple of Mithras, a monument to one of the Romans' most influential gods.

THE WILDFOWL AND WETLANDS CENTRE Washington, Tyne & Wear

The Wildfowl and Wetlands Centre at Washington is one of eight in Britain created and managed by the conservation organisation established by the eminent naturalist Sir Peter Scott.

The wetlands site here is now home to over 40 varieties of wild bird at any one time, usually including the largest concentration of mallard in the north east of England as well as wigeon, pochard, tufted duck, teal, redshank, heron and lapwing. Great spotted woodpeckers, sparrowhawks, bramblings and bullfinches are attracted in winter to feeding stations in areas of mature woodland.

The wildfowl collection includes over 1200 birds from more than 100 species. Some of the world's rarest and most colourful birds can be found here: among them is a flock of Chilean flamingoes.

Specially-built hides and observation towers mean that visitors can get close enough to the birds to feed, photograph or sketch them – or simply watch. Information boards and leaflets, and guided walks on some days, provide access to expert knowledge. Special events are run throughout the year, and the visitor centre contains a shop and refreshment facilities.

RABY CASTLE
Staindrop, near Darlington, County Durham

Though most of its interior now dates from the 18th and 19th centuries, the exterior of Raby Castle is still much as it was around 600 years earlier. Built for the powerful Nevill family, but confiscated by the monarch when they were on the losing side of the struggle to put Mary on the throne instead of Elizabeth I, Raby is now the home of Lord Barnard.

Set in a 270-acre park containing gardens, deer and two lakes, the fortress is built round a courtyard and encircled by a moat. Its nine distinctive towers all have names; the highest is the Clifford, 80 feet tall.

Inside, the Great Kitchen with its smoke-driven spit remains largely as it was when the castle was built. It was in daily use until recently, and now contains a collection of copper Victorian cooking utensils. The Baron's Hall, with its impressive beamed ceiling, recaptures the grandeur of another age, while the octagonal drawing room is a reminder of the more recent past. It is said to be the finest Victorian drawing room in England.

Carriages and other horse-drawn vehicles owned by the family are on display in the coach-houses, and visitors – welcome at specified times between March and September – can also enjoy the large walled gardens, complete with ancient yew hedges and 200-year-old fig tree.

The exterior of Raby Castle remains much the same as when it was built over 700 years ago.

ALNWICK *Northumberland*

Home for centuries of the powerful Percy family, the ancient market town of Alnwick (pronounced 'Annick') grew up around the 10th-century castle which is still the residence of the Duke and Duchess of Northumberland.

Throughout the turbulent Middle Ages, Alnwick was an important military stronghold. Devastated by the effects of Border warfare, its castle stood in ruins for 200 years before being restored by the dukes of Northumberland in the 18th and 19th centuries: architects Robert Adam and Anthony Salvin were involved in that project, and Capability Brown landscaped the grounds in 1765.

From the outside, Alnwick Castle still looks much as it must have done in the 14th century: its great walls, huge keep and many towers make it a spectacular sight. Rich collections of paintings, china and furniture adorn the interior. Visitors are welcome at specified times between the months of May and September.

Other castles (Warkworth and Dunstanburgh) and fortified houses (Elsdon and Preston Tower, for example) in the Alnwick area also testify to the region's turbulent medieval history, as do the battle sites at Otterburn, Hedgeley Moor, Homildon Hill, Halidon Hill and Flodden Field.

Alnwick is only four miles from a twenty-mile stretch of Heritage Coastline. Designated an Area of Outstanding Natural Beauty, the coastal scenery includes sweeping sands, rocky headlands, river estuaries and tiny havens.

West of the town lies glorious countryside crossed by networks of quiet roads. There are said to be more sheep here than people, and the peaceful valleys and rolling hills are ideal walking country. Local centres provide facilities for everything from guided walks to

The old cannon (above) at Alnwick Castle (below), is a reminder of the castle's importance as a military stronghold in the Middle Ages.

parachute jumping, hang-gliding to water-sports.

Alnwick's week-long medieval fair starts on the last Sunday in June; village shows, sheepdog trials and music festivals are held locally in July and August. The first weekend in November offers a feast of music-making and story-telling, when the region's musicians assemble for the Alnwick Northumberland Pipers Gathering.

THE NORTH OF ENGLAND OPEN AIR MUSEUM *Beamish, County Durham*

The early years of the 20th century are re-created — sights, sounds, smells and all — at the North of England Open Air Museum, Beamish.

Set in 300 acres of woodland and rolling countryside are Home Farm, the Old Town and the railway station, as well as the mine and its colliery community. Buildings from all over the north of England have been re-erected here to offer visitors the chance to experience life as it was lived almost a hundred years ago.

Shops are stocked with the goods that would have been on sale at the time; barrels of beer arrive at the local pub on a horse-drawn dray. The town's dentist and solicitor are at work, as is the teacher of pianoforte and singing. Women make mats, quilts and lace, and bake bread in coal-fired ovens. The vehicles of the time travel the streets and stop at the railway station; on some days a brass band plays in the park.

Everything — from the wallpaper in the dentist's parlour to the shorthorn cattle in the fields — is real.

Beamish is open year-round (except Mondays from November until Easter), though some areas may be closed in winter. Refreshments are available at the tea-rooms above the Co-op, and there is a pleasant picnic area. Cameras can be borrowed free of charge.

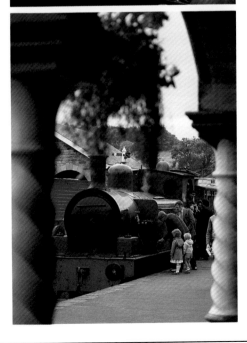

Capture the atmosphere of the early 20th century at the North of England Open Air Museum. Wander along the streets (top), visit the Co-op Hardware Shop (middle), or step onto the steam locomotive at Rowly Station.

An inscription on the entrance to the University Library at Durham (right).

DURHAM *County Durham*

Durham's Norman cathedral and castle dominate the town from their splendid setting high on a great sandstone outcrop almost encircled by the River Wear.

The cathedral is reckoned to be one of the finest in Europe and houses the remains of St Cuthbert, one of English Christianity's first saints, as well as the tomb of the Venerable Bede, writer of one of the earliest surviving English histories. The castle next to it, taking advantage of the superb natural protection

The city of Durham is almost encircled by the River Wear.

afforded by the River Wear's wooded gorge, became the centre of government for Durham's Prince Bishops, entrusted with king-like powers on behalf of England's monarchs for close on 800 years. Today, the castle is part of England's third-oldest university, and the wooded riverbanks are a picturesque backdrop for walking, fishing or a boat trip.

Durham's long history is celebrated at Durham University's Old Fulling Mill Museum of Archaeology, and at the Durham Heritage Centre in the 17th-century church of St Mary-le-Bow. The story of the University's development and its present-day activities are featured in the Old Library, Palace Yard.

Widening the scope from the local to the international, the only museum in Britain devoted to Oriental art collects together exhibits covering all the East's major cultures – from ancient Egypt through India, Tibet and China to Japan. Also part of the University is the eighteen-acre Botanic

Garden, featuring exotic specimens from places as far apart as America and the Himalayas as well as tropical plants and cacti.

Uncrowded roads lead out of the city to some of the highest, wildest and finest scenery in England. The Durham Dales – Teesdale, Weardale and the Derwent Valley – are less crowded than the better-known upland areas of the Pennine moors; walkers and anglers find them well worth exploring. Durham County Council organises over 200 walks a year, all led by experts, covering interests ranging from local history, archaeology and geology to ornithology, botany and farming: details from the Tourist Information Centre.

The 12th-century Treasury knocker, which criminals could clasp for sanctuary.

The south-east corner of Durham's Norman cathedral.

HIGH FORCE
Near Middleton-in-Teesdale, County Durham

The best time to see England's highest waterfall in full flow is during or after a rainy period. High Force is where the River Tees plunges 70 feet over the huge black cliff of the Great Whin Sill into a deep pool enclosed by rocks and shrubs.

Walkers will find other spectacular scenery in this area, which is part of the Raby Estate, five miles north-west of Middleton-in-Teesdale. Not far away, though harder to find, the Tees cascades about 200 feet down the dark, staircase-like rock formation known as Cauldron Snout.

There is a visitor centre at nearby Bowlees.

MORPETH CHANTRY BAGPIPE MUSEUM
Morpeth, Northumberland

Open all year, except around Christmas time, Morpeth Chantry Bagpipe Museum specialises in the history, development and music of the Northumbrian small pipes. Different from the better-known Scottish Pipes, and with a distinctive sound, the Northumbrian pipes are set here in the context of bagpipes the world over – from India to Inverness.

The pipes are brought to life with the help of a sound system which allows visitors to hear them by means of personal headphones.

The medieval chantry in which the museum is housed is in the centre of Morpeth, once an important cattle-market centre for the whole of northern England and Scotland. It is now a popular centre for travellers exploring the moors, hills and coast of Northumberland.

High Force Waterfall.

ST MARY'S LIGHTHOUSE
St Mary's Island, Whitley Bay, Northumberland

Originally part of a chain of lights that warned sailors away from the dangerous rocky coast, St Mary's Lighthouse is now a centre where visitors can learn about the lives of lighthouse-keepers as well as the wildlife of the area.

For two hours either side of high tide, the island on which it stands is inaccessible on foot because the causeway leading to it is submerged.

The 126-foot lighthouse was in service for almost a century before modern ship-based navigation methods made it redundant. What is now the Visitor Centre was once the home of the two keepers whose job it was to maintain the light – paraffin-fuelled until electrification in 1977. That a light was necessary at all is borne out by the number of wrecks said to lie along the stretch of coast between Blyth and Tynemouth – around 300 in all, relics from one of which still turn up in the rock pools on St Mary's Island in the shape of small green pebbles of apatite.

Visitors will still find a light at St Mary's, though it is no longer used for its original purpose.

The rocks of St Mary's Island are home to a rich variety of wildlife. Over 70 kinds of seaweed have been found here, and the rock pools provide havens for molluscs like limpets, mussels and winkles. Crabs, starfish and tentacled sea-anemones can also be seen here.

Visitors can learn about the lives of lighthouse keepers at St Mary's Lighthouse.

PRESTON PARK MUSEUM
Stockton-on-Tees, Cleveland

Preston Park Museum has been designed to give visitors a taste of Victorian England, and the 100-acre park in which it is set hosts a wealth of events throughout the year.

Preston Hall, built in 1825, now houses an extensive museum. Among its exhibits are collections of pewter, arms and armour, costume, snuff boxes and children's toys. Galleries throughout the Hall show life as it was in Victorian times, and the re-creation of

Preston Hall recreates Victorian England in its period rooms and its china shop.

a typical Victorian high street features period shops and working craftsmen. There are regular demonstrations by skilled craftsmen and folk musicians.

A section of trackbed from the world's first passenger railway – the Stockton & Darlington, opened in 1825 – runs through the park. It now forms the basis of an attractive walk, and is the central feature of the Stockton Railway Heritage Trail. Visitors are free to explore the peaceful riverside and woodland walks throughout the park; fishing, crazy golf and pitch-and-putt are also on offer. There are fully-equipped play areas for children.

Preston Park is the venue for the annual Historical Vehicle Rally, one of the largest get-togethers in the north of England for lovers and owners of veteran and vintage motors. Folk music festivals, a fair and a family fun run also appear on the programme.

KILLHOPE WHEEL LEADMINING CENTRE Upper Weardale, County Durham

Set in the heart of the North Pennines Area of Outstanding Natural Beauty is Britain's most complete leadmining site. From the late 18th to the mid-19th century, this area was to lead what the Klondike was to gold; now Durham County Council has restored Killhope's lead mine and crushing mill so that present-day visitors can experience what it was like to work there.

Displays in what were the miners' sleeping quarters tell the story of mining in the area, and visitors can actually explore the site, pan for lead in the stream, and work the machinery under the guidance of a member of staff.

Killhope is open daily from 10.30am to 5pm between Easter and the end of October. In November and March, parties can visit as long as they have booked in advance; guided tours should also be booked beforehand.

GATESHEAD METROCENTRE
Gateshead, Tyne & Wear

MetroCentre is Europe's largest out-of-town shopping and leisure centre. Three miles of tree-lined shopping malls are all under cover and temperature-controlled; parking for over 10,000 cars is free, and the centre is well serviced by public transport. Along with more than 350 shops, MetroCentre has a ten-screen cinema, a 28-lane bowling centre, over 50 places to eat – and MetroLand, with

fairground rides and a host of other attractions.

MetroCentre's shopping facilities include all the major British high-street chain stores, as well as smaller specialist shops. Banks, building societies, estate agents and travel agents are also represented. 'Themed' shopping areas – the Mediterranean Village, Roman Forum, Garden Court and Antique Village – create their own atmosphere. Throughout MetroCentre, the shops are open until 8pm on weekdays (9pm on Thursdays).

Eating places cater for every taste, whether the need is for a gourmet meal or a quick snack. Mexican, Italian, Spanish, Greek and Thai food is on offer, as is traditional British fare. Late-evening opening is a feature of many venues, and some are open on Sundays.

The multi-screen cinema and bowling centre are both open seven days a week. So is MetroLand, with its fairground rides, video games, nine-hole mini-golf course and Wizard's Castle all set in the fantasy kingdom of King Wiz, landscaped with waterfalls, streams and clouds. Entry to MetroLand is free, but the various attractions each have their own charges.

Covering an expanse of three miles, Gateshead MetroCentre is Europe's largest out-of-town shopping and leisure centre.

The Heatherslaw Light Railway (opposite page) takes visitors along the banks of the River Till. Bamburgh Castle (opposite page) is dramatically perched on a crag beside the sea.

THE BOWES MUSEUM
Barnard Castle, County Durham

Barnard Castle is probably the last place anyone would expect to find a glorious 19th-century French château crammed with treasures from all over Europe. It is, however, where John Bowes − local landowner, MP, industrialist, race-horse owner, theatre-lover and collector − built the museum named after him and where he and his wife,

Barnard Castle (right, and below) houses the magnificent Bowes Museum which is full of wonderful treasures from all over Europe.

a Parisian actress and painter, displayed their collections of *objets d'art*.

Put together in only fifteen years, specifically for public enjoyment, the Bowes' collections include paintings by El Greco, Goya, Boucher, Corbet, Sassetta and Tiepolo. French 18th-century furniture and tapestries are among the objects displayed in period settings. More recent additions include English furniture, silver, costume, toys, and local antiquities.

The Bowes Museum stands in a 21-acre landscaped park complete with gardens, bowling greens and tennis courts which are open to the public. The museum itself can be visited all year round, except for a week at Christmas time.

Sited on a cliff overlooking the River Tees, the town of Barnard Castle is an attractive centre from which to explore Teesdale. Two major literary figures certainly thought it worth a visit: Sir Walter Scott found inspiration for *Rokeby* in the castle's 14th-century Round Tower and, in 1838, Charles Dickens stayed at the town's King's Head Hotel while writing *Nicholas Nickleby*.

THE HEATHERSLAW LIGHT RAILWAY
Etal, Northumberland

Travel along the banks of the River Till from Heatherslaw Mill to Etal Castle on a 15-inch gauge steam railway. The 3½-mile round trip starts every 40 minutes between the hours of 10am and 6pm, April to October, and by appointment during the winter months.

Heatherslaw is not far from the medieval battle site of Flodden Field. Etal Castle, a crumbling ruin at one end of Etal's street of thatched cottages, was destroyed in 1496 by James IV of Scotland. All that remains now is the south-east gate tower, and a portion of curtain wall with parts of two other towers.

Free parking is available at the light railway's Heatherslaw Terminus, and the John Sinclair Railway Museum is on site here, too. Nearby is Heatherslaw Corn Mill, a working 19th-century water-driven mill which, water-levels permitting, grinds every day.

BAMBURGH CASTLE
Bamburgh, Northumberland

Dramatically sited on a 150-foot precipice overlooking the sea, Bamburgh Castle was once an important border stronghold and the seat of the kings of Northumbria.

Extensively restored in the 19th century, the red sandstone castle dominates the sleepy village in which it is situated. It now contains important collections of arms and armour, china, porcelain and furniture as well as tapestries and paintings. Guns on the upper terraces of the castle still point out to sea.

The castle affords fine views of the Farne Islands, $4\frac{1}{2}$ miles out to sea. Once an important religious centre, the islands are now breeding-grounds for young seabirds and have been designated an Area of Outstanding Natural Beauty.

St Aidan, who died in Bamburgh in 651, is commemorated by a fine Norman church. Also remembered here is local heroine Grace Darling who, with her father, braved foul weather and mountainous seas in a tiny rowing boat to rescue nine survivors from the paddle-steamer *Forfarshire*, wrecked on the rocky Farnes in 1838. Her elaborate memorial is in St Aidan's churchyard, and the nearby Grace Darling Museum contains reminders of her heroic exploit — including the boat involved in the rescue.

NEWCASTLE-UPON-TYNE Tyne & Wear

Newcastle-upon-Tyne began life as a Roman fort on Hadrian's Wall. The new castle after which the city is named was built by the Normans on the same site: its keep and gatehouse remain, and now house the Castle Keep and Black Gate museums.

Though reckoned to be the third most prosperous town in Britain by the 14th century, Newcastle's real boom came 500 years later with its development as a centre for ship-building and heavy engineering. The fine city centre buildings in the unique 'Tyneside Classical' style date from this period; the award-winning Civic Centre, opened in 1968, confirmed that the city's 20th-century planners are no less innovative than their predecessors.

Newcastle's Central Station is one of the great monuments to the railway age. When it was finished in 1865, it covered seventeen acres and had two miles of platforms. George and Robert Stephenson built the locomotive 'Rocket' near here; examples of their work, and that of the city's other brilliant engineers — between them responsible for the hydraulic crane, the steam turbine, and the incandescent light bulb — are collected in the Museum of Science and Engineering. Over 80 full-sized engines are displayed there.

Seven bridges carry road and rail links across the River Tyne: the oldest designed by Robert Stephenson, and one of the newest built for the city's Metro. Past and present come together on the quayside, an area which is becoming increasingly interesting as regeneration progresses and small shops, restaurants and businesses establish themselves. There is an open-air market here on Sunday mornings.

Though the city's development has been dominated by heavy industry, Newcastle is also an important cultural centre. Theatres offer year-round programmes of entertainment, and there are thriving annual festivals of youth arts (June–July), film (September–October) and jazz (May). The largest travelling fair in Europe, The Hoppings, arrives at Newcastle's Town Moor at the end of June. Sporting attractions include regular horse-racing at Gosforth Racecourse, and the annual Great North Run, in which around 25,000 competitors cover the half-marathon distance to South Shields (June).

FOR FURTHER INFORMATION CONTACT:

Tourist Information Centre
Market Place
DURHAM
County Durham DH1 3NJ
Telephone: (091) 384 3720

Tourist Information Centre
Monk Street
NEWCASTLE-UPON-TYNE
Tyne & Wear NE1 4XW
Telephone: (091) 261 0691

Northumbria Tourist Board
Aykley Heads
DURHAM
County Durham DH1 5UX
Telephone: (091) 384 6905

Four bridges across the River Tyne.

NEWCASTLE-UPON-TYNE

The Eldon Square shopping centre (above); the Civic Centre (above, right); a reflection of Emerson's Chambers in a contemporary building (right); and dancers from the Aurea School of Dancing.

SCOTLAND

Eilean Donan Castle, Loch Duich.

The sheer mountains and misty lochs of Scotland are complemented by its ruined abbeys, great defensive castles, and fortifications, which litter the great nature reserves and craggy landscapes, harking back to the country's bloody and romantic past.

Most of Scotland's population live in the lowland belt running from east to west. This land divides the lower Tweedsmuir and the Cheviot Hills in the south and the high region of the Grampian and Cairngorm Mountains in the north. It is here that Ben Nevis stands at 4406 feet – the highest mountain in the British Isles.

The area is unspoilt and rugged. In the north the many lochs include the legendary Loch Ness and off the north and west coasts are the Hebrides, Isle of Aran, Orkneys and Shetland islands. In the mountains live red and roe deer, mountain goats, the wildcat and the rare golden eagle. To the south are coastal cliffs, gently rolling Cheviot hills, the Eden valley and the Kielder Forest of the Border Country. This area has been fought over for centuries and remains of past skirmishes include the Border peel towers at Smailholm and Preston and the famous Hadrian's Wall.

Edinburgh is one of the world's most attractive capitals and the many elegant buildings include a castle perched on a crag rising 443 feet above sea level; Princes Street running straight through the city; and the Palace of Holyroodhouse – officially the residence of the Queen of Scotland. The city is interlaced with gardens that give a sudden profusion of colour, amid grey stone streets.

Scotland's second city is Glasgow which was founded in the 6th century. Today Glasgow is Europe's cultural centre and has over 35 museums and galleries. The city includes Strathclyde University where John Logie Baird – the inventor of television – once studied.

Sheep farming is particularly important in the border hills, where the wool is used to manufacture traditional tartan and tweeds, as well as woollen jumpers. A number of woollen mills are open to the public.

The area is the homeland of scotch whisky and the birthplace of the famous Edinburgh rock. The coastline is dotted with fishing villages and landlocked bays and smoked fish is a speciality of the area. Other traditional dishes include haggis, shortbread and porridge.

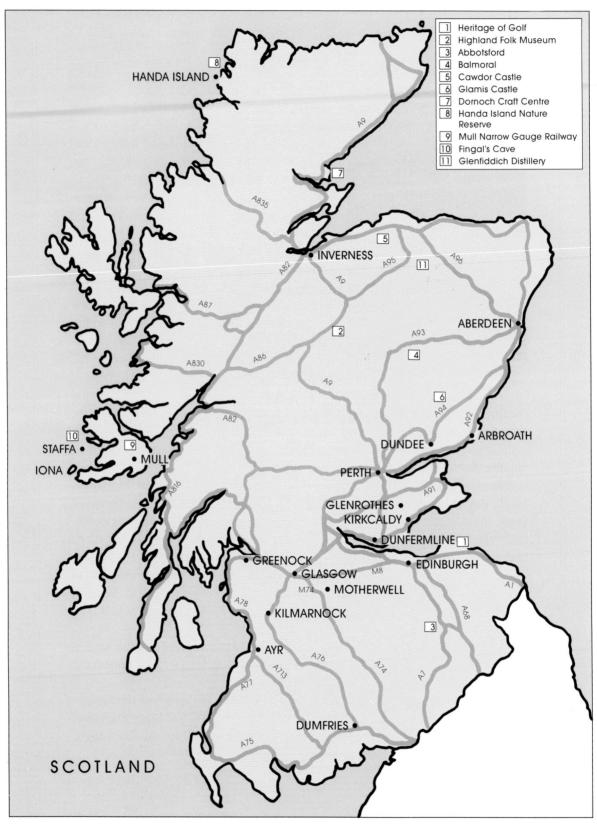

1	Heritage of Golf
2	Highland Folk Museum
3	Abbotsford
4	Balmoral
5	Cawdor Castle
6	Glamis Castle
7	Dornoch Craft Centre
8	Handa Island Nature Reserve
9	Mull Narrow Gauge Railway
10	Fingal's Cave
11	Glenfiddich Distillery

HANDA ISLAND 8

A9

A835

7

INVERNESS 5

A82 A9 A95 11 A96

A87

2 A93 ABERDEEN

A830 A86 4

A9 6

A82 A94 A92

10 9 ARBROATH
STAFFA MULL DUNDEE
IONA

PERTH A91

GLENROTHES
KIRKCALDY

A816 DUNFERMLINE 1

GREENOCK EDINBURGH
GLASGOW M8 A1
M74 MOTHERWELL
A78 KILMARNOCK A68

3 A74 A7
AYR A76
A713
A77

DUMFRIES

A75

SCOTLAND

THE GLENFIDDICH DISTILLERY
Dufftown, Banffshire

Since the first drops of malt whisky ran from its stills on Christmas Day, 1887, five generations of the Grant family have owned and managed the Glenfiddich Distillery. Glenfiddich is unique: the only Highland malt to be bottled where it is made from malted barley mixed with pure Highland spring water.

Guided tours of the Distillery start in its theatre, where an audiovisual presentation introduces the history of Scotch whisky. Then visitors can experience the whole process that leads from barley to bottle – from the Mash House, where barley and water are brought together, to the Tun Room for fermentation, and then to the Stillhouse where the whisky is fermented twice in traditionally-shaped stills made by the distillery's own coppersmiths. Visitors follow its progress into oak casks and the warehouse, where the spirit lies undisturbed until it is mature enough to embark on the final stage of its journey to the bottling hall.

Tours end with the opportunity to taste the finished product in the Malt Barn . . .

Visitors are welcome on weekdays (excluding Christmas and New Year holidays) all year round, plus Saturdays and Sunday afternoons between Easter and mid-October.

THE HERITAGE OF GOLF
Gullane, East Lothian

Golf is an ancient game, and its origins are obscure. It is thought to have been brought to Scotland centuries ago from Holland, possibly by soldiers or sailors who travelled between the two countries, and played first on links near Scotland's east-coast ports where the habits of rabbits and sheep determined the varying lengths of grass still characteristic of today's courses.

Golf's fascinating history encompasses balls made from boiled feathers and individually-crafted clubs shaped by bowmakers and carpenters. Early players wore swallow-tailed red coats, even the occasional top hat; practical waterproofs and spiked shoes are a relatively recent innovation. The Heritage of Golf exhibitions cover the evolution of clubs, balls and costume from golf's early days to the present, and the personalities – players, caddies and club-makers – whose presence has enriched the game over the years are also featured.

Open by appointment to individuals or

The still house at Glenfiddich Distillery, where whisky has been produced for over a century.

groups of fewer than ten people, The Heritage of Golf displays are designed to appeal to anyone who enjoys the game. Historians, collectors or knowledgeable addicts may well find that it takes longer than the usual half-an-hour or so to explore all the memorabilia on show. All are welcome to buy their own memento from a selection that ranges from postcards through tee-pegs to old clubs costing between £25 and £2500.

HIGHLAND FOLK MUSEUM Kingussie, Inverness-shire

Though the traditional Highland way of life is fast disappearing from modern Scotland, the Highland Folk Museum is doing its part to ensure that it is not forgotten.

Indoor and outdoor exhibits combine to show how the Highlands' inhabitants – all the way back to Picts, Celts and Vikings – managed to adapt their cultures to the area's natural environment and its resources.

The open air museum features a reconstruction of one of the black houses so typical of the Isle of Lewis. Low and thick-walled, its design and construction was influenced by the island's prevailing climate as well as the needs of the people – and animals – who lived in it. Also from Lewis is an example of the Viking-influenced Norse Mill, a little water-driven mill introduced into Scotland during medieval times.

Housed in other buildings around the museum site are exhibitions of the farming implements used over the years in the Highlanders' struggle for subsistence, re-creations of rooms in their homes, and collections of musical instruments and costume.

The Highland Folk Museum is open daily from April through October, and weekdays only between November and March. Opening times vary with the time of year.

CAWDOR CASTLE Nairn, Nairnshire

Shakespeare's Macbeth was Thane of Cawdor, and the noblemen bearing that name have lived in Cawdor Castle for over 600 years. It is still the home of Lord and Lady Cawdor today.

The castle's central tower was built in 1372, fortified almost 100 years later, and surrounded by other buildings in the 16th century. Despite the fact that it is home to a 20th-century family, its medieval origins are evident in its ancient stonework, low doorways, winding staircases and deep-set windows. The tapestries so essential for warmth still adorn thick walls.

Visitors are welcome at Cawdor Castle daily from the beginning of May to the end of September. Beautiful gardens surround the castle, and there are a number of nature trails in the grounds as well as mini-golf and a putting green, picnic areas, a snack bar and licensed restaurant.

BALMORAL CASTLE Aberdeenshire

When Queen Victoria and Prince Albert bought the Balmoral estate in 1853, the present castle had not yet been built. The original 'Bouchmorale', Gaelic for 'majestic dwelling', existed as long ago as 1484, but it was rebuilt as a castle mansion in the Scottish Baronial style and has now been the British Royal Family's holiday home for over a century.

Balmoral's grounds are open every day

The 'Harrowing Lady' at Highland Folk Museum.

The Royal Family's holiday home at Balmoral Castle is set amongst wooded hills on a curve of the salmon-filled River Dee.

(except Sundays) during May, June and July, as is the ballroom where paintings and works of art are on show. Those planning a visit are advised to find out in advance whether members of the Royal Family are in residence, as members of the public may not be admitted then.

Also during May, June and July, experienced pony-riders over the age of twelve can take part in guided treks through Balmoral's grounds and forests, on the estate's own ponies. These must be booked in advance.

Not far away is Craithie Church, built in 1895 and the Royal Family's place of worship when they are in residence. It contains many Royal memorials.

GLASGOW Strathclyde

Surrounded by coalfields and only twenty miles from the sea, Glasgow prospered and grew rapidly during the years of Britain's Industrial Revolution, though it had been a major port since the 17th century. Two hundred years on, Scotland's largest city was dominated by heavy industry, ship-building, and the notorious tenements built to provide cheap housing for the massive workforce. Glasgow has seen hard times in recent years as traditional industries and working practices have been replaced, but is currently undergoing something of a renaissance.

Selected to follow Athens, Florence, Amsterdam, Berlin and Paris as European City of Culture (1990), Glasgow ranks as one of the world's finest centres for the visual and performing arts. It is home to the Scottish Opera, Scottish Ballet, the Scottish National Orchestra, the Citizens Theatre and the Royal Scottish Academy of Music and Drama. Year-round programmes featuring these and other major performers are presented by theatres and concert halls throughout the city.

Outstanding museums and art galleries, of which there are several, contain both general and specialised collections. Britain's finest civic array of British and European paintings can be found at the Glasgow Art Gallery and Museum; the Hunterian Art Gallery, part of Glasgow's university, displays paintings by Rembrandt and Rubens, and houses an internationally-known collection of Whistler's work as well as 19th- and 20th-century Scottish paintings. Local and social history are covered by the Barony Chambers at the Auld Kirk Museum and the People's Palace, as well as a number of smaller museums at locations in and around the city.

Haggs Castle is a 400-year-old museum designed with children in mind; the recently-enlarged Museum of Transport includes a reconstruction of a 1938 Glasgow street, displays of post-1930s cars, and collections of all sorts of wheeled vehicles designed for a range of purposes.

Much of Glasgow's finest architecture reflects its Victorian prosperity, though its 12th-century cathedral bears witness to the city's medieval origins. Its importance as a trading centre in the 17th and 18th centuries is remembered in the Merchant City quarter, while later influences include that of Art Nouveau artist and architect James Rennie Mackintosh, whose Glasgow School of Art is reckoned to be a masterpiece of the Modern movement.

Sporting facilities in and around Glasgow are impressive, while parks and open spaces – 6000 acres of them – offer a range of leisure amenities. Within the city itself are the 42-acre Botanic Gardens (specially famous for its collections of begonias and orchids), Queen's Park (named for Mary, Queen of Scots, and renowned for fine floral displays) and Victoria Park, where the Fossil Grove features the stumps and roots of trees that grew 330 million years ago. Not far away are country parks – Castle Semple, Muirshiel and the RSPB reserve at Lochwinnoch; Drumpellier and Dunbeth at Coatbridge – each with their own range of attractions ranging from water-sports to woodland walks, nature trails to traditional park games.

GLASGOW

Glasgow's wealth of interest earned it the status of 1990 European City of Culture. The Stock Exchange at George Place (above); George Square (above, right); the 12th-century cathedral, and statue of the explorer David Livingstone who studied at Glasgow University (below, right); and the River Clyde (below).

ABBOTSFORD Melrose, Borders

Sir Walter Scott, one of Scotland's best-known writers, bought the 110-acre estate where Abbotsford now stands for 4000 guineas in 1811. It was a farm then, called Cartley Hall, and Scott began his series of Waverley novels there in 1814.

As he became more successful, he bought more land to add to the estate, and by 1820 he had extended it to around 1400 acres. Two years later, he had Cartley Hall demolished and the present imposing mansion was built. Scott died here in 1832.

The entrance hall at Abbotsford (below).

Though later members of the family added Abbotsford's west wing, entrance lodge and terraces, the house is still much the same as it was in its first owner's day.

Scott was a passionate collector of historic relics, including armour and weapons. These are on display to today's visitors, as are his study, drawing room, entrance hall and dining room. Scott's library, with over 9000 rare volumes, is also on view.

Set in glorious countryside, and surrounded by extensive gardens, Abbotsford is open to the public between late March and the end of October.

ABERDEEN Grampian

Old Aberdeen, a thriving port by the end of the 13th century, was largely burnt to the ground in 1336 by England's Edward III. From its ashes, a new city rose, though some of the old town's cobbled streets and pink granite houses can still be seen today.

Outstanding buildings in Old Aberdeen include twin-towered St Machar's, one of the city's three cathedrals, now used as a parish church; St Andrew's Episcopalian Cathedral; and King's College, the university of Old Aberdeen, founded in 1494. One of the oldest bridges in Britain is here, too: the Brig o' Balgownie, with its clusters of 16th-century cottages, spanning the River Don with a 62-foot arch completed around 1320.

Modern Aberdeen dates from the end of the 18th century, when a wealth of handsome neo-Classical buildings, made of grey granite flecked with mica that sparkles in the sun, sprang up alongside the old town. It is now the largest fishing-port in Scotland (visit the fishmarket early in the morning to watch the catch being unloaded and auctioned), as well as a major commercial and industrial centre with strong links with the North Sea oil industry.

Though often called Scotland's 'Granite City', a name suggesting harsh, drab austerity, Aberdeen has won the prestigious 'Britain in Bloom' trophy many times and

His Majesty's Theatre at Aberdeen (below, left) and Duthie Park Winter Gardens (below).

has become famous for its roses. Four million are said to bloom here every summer, and the city holds a Rose Festival in August.

Aberdeen's heritage is celebrated at a number of fine museums and galleries. Notable among them are James Dun's House, a children's museum where Victorian toys are displayed alongside treasures from Scottish history; the folk museum at the 16th-century Provost Skene's House; and the Maritime Museum, where models, paintings, displays and audiovisual presentations tell of Aberdeen's shipbuilding, fishing and oil-related industries. The Maritime Museum is based in one of the city's oldest buildings, Provost Ross's House in Shiprow, thought to be Aberdeen's oldest street. Marischal College houses an anthropological museum, while Aberdeen Art Gallery shows permanent collections of 18th-, 19th- and 20th-century works with an emphasis on contemporary art.

Theatres, cinemas, parks and gardens – as well as excellent facilities for a number of indoor and outdoor sports – are all featured in a number of detailed brochures available from the Tourist Information Centre. Also published is a monthly *What's On* guide to current entertainment.

Aberdeen's year-round programme of special events and festivals includes the city's Spring Flower Show (March), concert programmes presented by the Scottish Chamber and National orchestras (April), the Granite City Car Rally (May), Aberdeen Highland Games (June), and an Arts Carnival (July). August brings the city's Fish Festival, International Youth Festival and

A beach on the tiny island of Iona.

Rose Festival; alternative music is celebrated in October, and Christmas shopping is the main attraction in November and December.

IONA *Inner Hebrides*

It was to Iona that St Columba came from Ireland in the 6th century, to found a monastery and establish Christianity in Scotland. From this tiny island spread the learning, Celtic art and influence on the kingdoms of Scotland that first made Iona famous. It has been a place of pilgrimage ever since, and many early Scottish kings and chieftains are buried here.

Iona's Abbey, with its distinctive architecture and peaceful cloisters, was founded by medieval Benedictine monks, and has been restored this century. Everywhere on the island there are reminders of the religious figures, poets and artists who have been inspired by its atmosphere.

Iona's beauty and tranquillity are also a magnet to nature-lovers: birdwatchers, botanists and geologists find plenty of interest here.

Limited numbers of people wishing to stay on Iona, rather than simply visit it via one of the regular ferry-crossings from Oban and Fort William, can actually spend a week living in the Abbey and joining in one of the programmes organised by the Iona Community.

MULL *Inner Hebrides*

Mull is the second largest of the Inner Hebrides, the group of islands off Scotland's west coast that includes Skye (the largest), Iona and Staffa as well as Eigg and Rhum.

In addition to its scenic beauty, Mull is famous for its Little Theatre whose 38 seats make it the smallest professional theatre in the country. Beautifully situated on a hillside, Mull Little Theatre mounts live performances every year from Easter to October for which fast-selling seats can be booked in advance. The Theatre Restaurant specialises in fresh local produce, the menu changes daily, and it is open to both theatregoers and those only wishing to dine.

Victorian Torosay Castle with its magnificent gardens is at the end of the twenty-minute journey by narrow-gauge railway that starts its regular scheduled services from Craignure (Old Pier) Station. Steam and diesel-hauled trains travel $1\frac{1}{4}$ miles along the $10\frac{1}{4}$-inch track, through woodland with superb mountain and sea views.

Caledonian MacBrayne car ferries sail regularly to Mull from Oban and Lochaline on the mainland.

FINGAL'S CAVE AND STAFFA
Inner Hebrides

Romantic and uninhabited, Staffa is famous for its extraordinary rock formations and remarkable caves. One of them, Fingal's Cave, has been immortalised by the composer Mendelssohn in his *Hebrides* overture and, with its cluster columns and a symmetry so precise it looks man-made, it has a cathedral-like majesty. Those affected by its splendour have included Queen Victoria and Prince Albert, the artist Turner and writers Keats, Wordsworth, Tennyson and Scott.

Weather permitting, Staffa is accessible by boat. Day-trips from Oban and Fort William take in Mull and Iona as well as Staffa; visitors staying on Mull or Iona can join one of the regular cruises to Staffa.

GLAMIS CASTLE Angus

There has been a castle at Glamis since the 14th century, though the present château-style one dates from some 300 years later. It was the childhood home of Her Majesty

The smallest professional theatre in the country can be found at Dervaig on the Island of Mull (above).
Fingal's Cave at Staffa (below).

Glamis Castle (above) was the childhood home of Her Majesty Queen Elizabeth the Queen Mother. A portrait of the Queen Mother (below) when she was Duchess of York.

Gardens surrounding the castle reflect the changing tastes of landscape designers over the centuries. Although Capability Brown's 18th-century influence is much in evidence, older types of garden layout have gradually been reintroduced, especially in the Dutch and Italian gardens.

A ³/₄-mile nature trail through the grounds starts near the Italian Garden, the former Butler's Pantry is now the Castle Gift Shop, and the West Turret's Gallery Shop sells pictures, prints and antiques.

Glamis Castle is open to the public at Easter, then on afternoons from the beginning of May to the end of September.

Queen Elizabeth The Queen Mother; her younger daughter, Princess Margaret, was born here in 1930. Members of the Lyon family, later created Earls of Strathmore and Kinghorne, have lived here since 1372 – and they still do.

The romance of Glamis Castle stems not only from its fairy-tale appearance, but from the long history and famous people associated with it. Its beautiful rooms are adorned with fine furniture and other reminders of previous occupants: some grand, some intimate. Collections of china, paintings and tapestry are also on view. Shakespeare's *Macbeth* links Glamis with Cawdor: King Malcolm's Room and Duncan's Hall at Glamis commemorate the connection.

EDINBURGH Lothian

Built on spectacular hills and valleys, Scotland's capital is famed for its elegant classical architecture, panoramic views and open spaces. Dominating the city's skyline is Edinburgh Castle, built on a volcanic outcrop and dating from the 12th century. The Scottish crown jewels are here, and standing within its grounds is St Margaret's Chapel, the city's oldest building.

Running down through Edinburgh's medieval Old Town, from the castle to the Palace of Holyroodhouse, is the Royal Mile, where picturesque closes house a variety of small museums, craft shops, pubs and restaurants. Edinburgh's 18th-century New Town lies immediately to the north of the Old, and boasts fine Georgian buildings, tree-lined squares and crescents linked by wide, handsome streets.

Museums and art galleries abound. In the Old Town's narrow, winding streets around the base of Castle Rock are Huntly House (a reconstructed 16th-century town house, containing the city's local history museum), the Museum of Childhood and the People's Story Museum in the Canongate Tolbooth, where a former prison now houses exhibits telling of the lives, work and pastimes of

Edinburgh's citizens from the late 18th century to the present. The National Gallery of Scotland, the Royal Scottish Academy, the Scottish National Gallery of Modern Art and the Scottish National Portrait Gallery all house impressive collections in equally impressive surroundings, while the modern City Art Centre presents a variety of temporary exhibitions.

Highlight of Edinburgh's cultural year is the Edinburgh International Festival. During the last three weeks of August the city hosts musical, operatic, ballet and theatrical events from all over the world while, running parallel to the official Festival, the Fringe attracts an eclectic mix of less well-known artistes. The Military Tattoo, Edinburgh International Film Festival and Jazz Festival also take place during this period.

Edinburgh offers more, however, than a three-week orgy of summertime cultural entertainment. Off-season highlights include international rugby union matches during the winter, the Folk Festival in March, and the Royal Highland Show in June; New Year's Eve – Hogmanay – is the excuse for celebrations all over Scotland.

Shoppers and souvenir hunters are well catered for, as are antique-lovers and buyers of old books. Those in search of physical rather than intellectual pleasures will find plenty of facilities in the city's sports centres, swimming pools – and even a dry ski slope – as well as in the numerous parks offering the chance to bowl or play tennis. There are 24 golf courses within the city boundaries.

Within easy reach of the glorious walking country of the Pentland Hills, Edinburgh itself has plenty of open spaces. The Royal Botanic Garden, Britain's second oldest, boasts the largest collection of spring-flowering rhododendrons in the UK. Holyrood Park, once the private grounds of the Palace of Holyroodhouse – Her Majesty the Queen Mother's official Scottish residence – is now open to the public.

Edinburgh Castle and the annual military tattoo.

FOR FURTHER INFORMATION CONTACT:

Tourist Information Centre
St Nicholas House
Broad Street
ABERDEEN AB9 1DE
Telephone: (0224) 632727

Tourist Information Centre
Waverley Market
Princes Street
EDINBURGH EH2 2QP
Telephone: (031) 557 1700

Tourist Information Centre
35 St Vincent Place
GLASGOW G1 2ER
Telephone: (041) 227 4880

Scottish Tourist Board
23 Ravelston Terrace
EDINBURGH EH4 3EU
Telephone: (031) 332 2433

• INDEX •